THE VISUAL DICTIONARY *of* HUMAN ANATOMY

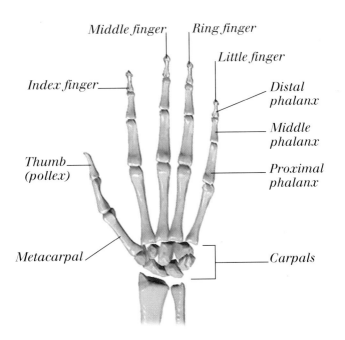

Middle finger   Ring finger

Index finger

Little finger

Distal phalanx

Middle phalanx

Thumb (pollex)

Proximal phalanx

Metacarpal

Carpals

BONES OF THE HAND

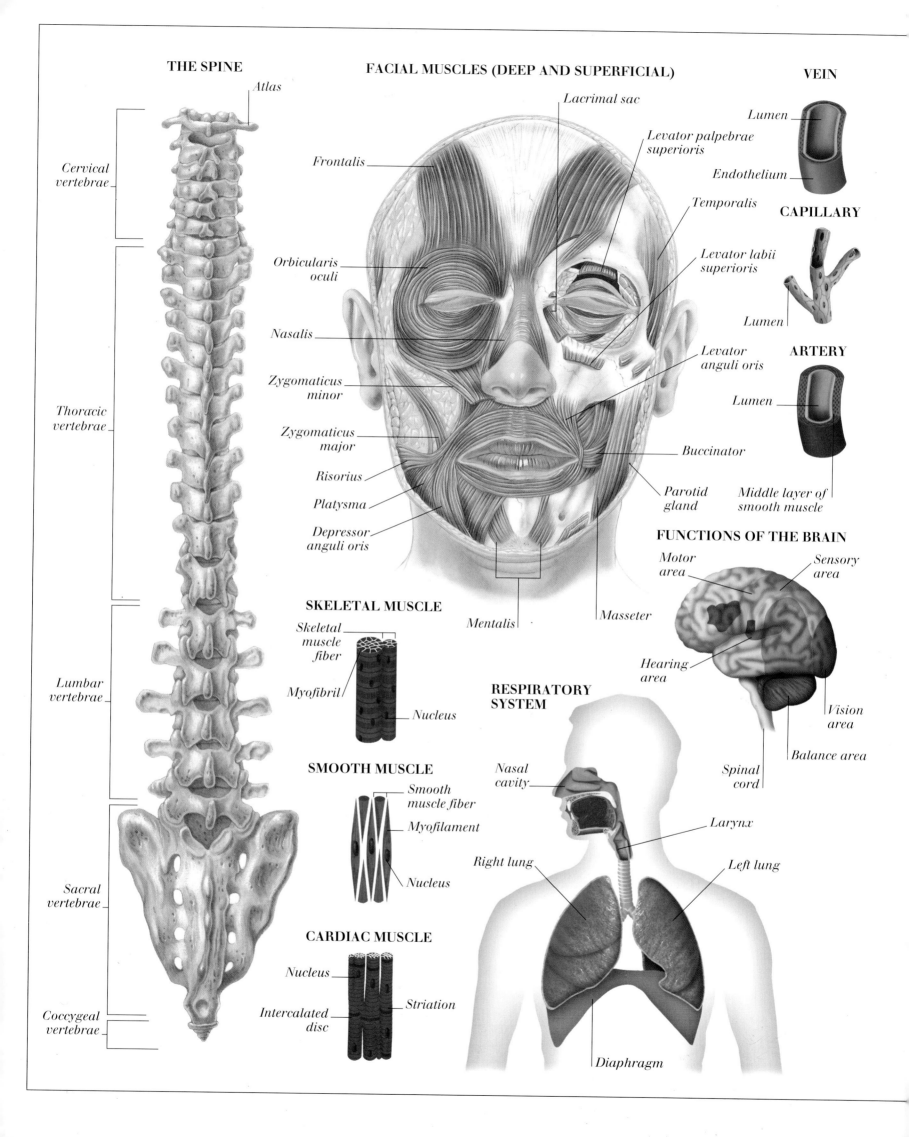

THE SPINE

Atlas

Cervical vertebrae

Thoracic vertebrae

Lumbar vertebrae

Sacral vertebrae

Coccygeal vertebrae

FACIAL MUSCLES (DEEP AND SUPERFICIAL)

Lacrimal sac

Levator palpebrae superioris

Frontalis

Temporalis

Levator labii superioris

Orbicularis oculi

Levator anguli oris

Nasalis

Zygomaticus minor

Zygomaticus major

Buccinator

Risorius

Parotid gland

Middle layer of smooth muscle

Platysma

Depressor anguli oris

Mentalis

Masseter

VEIN

Lumen

Endothelium

CAPILLARY

Lumen

ARTERY

Lumen

FUNCTIONS OF THE BRAIN

Motor area

Sensory area

Hearing area

Vision area

Balance area

Spinal cord

SKELETAL MUSCLE

Skeletal muscle fiber

Myofibril

Nucleus

SMOOTH MUSCLE

Smooth muscle fiber

Myofilament

Nucleus

CARDIAC MUSCLE

Nucleus

Striation

Intercalated disc

RESPIRATORY SYSTEM

Nasal cavity

Larynx

Right lung

Left lung

Diaphragm

THE VISUAL
DICTIONARY *of*
HUMAN
ANATOMY

STRUCTURE OF A LYMPH NODE

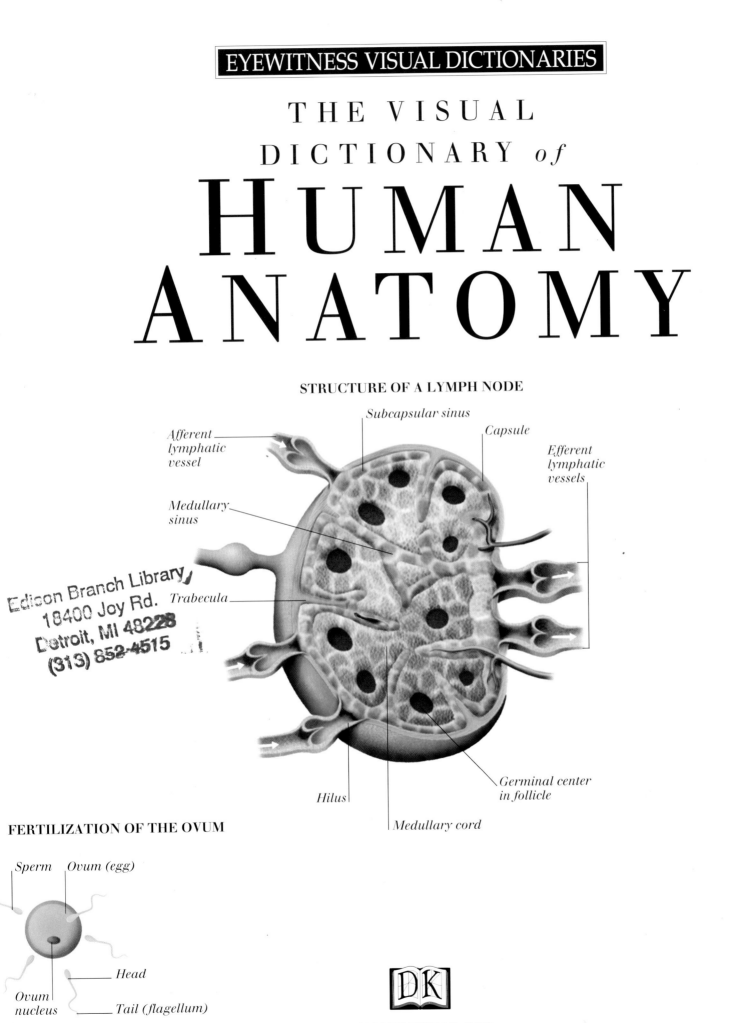

Subcapsular sinus

Capsule

Afferent lymphatic vessel

Efferent lymphatic vessels

Medullary sinus

Trabecula

Germinal center in follicle

Hilus

Medullary cord

FERTILIZATION OF THE OVUM

Sperm Ovum (egg)

Head

Ovum nucleus

Tail (flagellum)

DK

DK PUBLISHING, INC

A DK PUBLISHING BOOK

ART EDITOR PAUL GREENLEAF
CONSULTANT EDITOR DR. RICHARD WALKER
PROJECT EDITORS KIRSTIE HILLS, PHILIPPA COLVIN
EDITOR DES REID
DESIGN ASSISTANT STEPHEN CROUCHER
US EDITOR CONSTANCE M. ROBINSON
US CONSULTANT JEFFEREY KAUFMANN

DEPUTY ART DIRECTOR TINA VAUGHAN
MANAGING EDITOR SEAN MOORE
SENIOR ART EDITOR TRACY HAMBLETON-MILES
SENIOR EDITOR LOUISE CANDLISH

ILLUSTRATIONS RICHARD TIBBITTS, PHILIP WILSON,
HALLI VERRINDER, ALISON BROWN,
JOANNA CAMERON, MICK GILLAH, GARETH WILD

PRODUCTION STEPHEN STUART

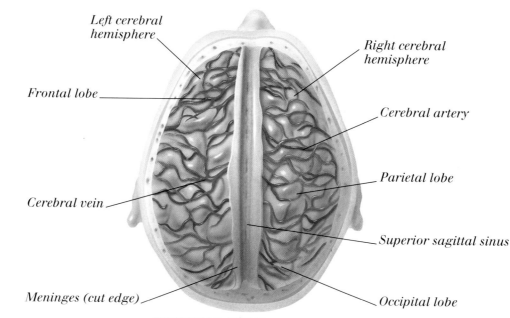

Left cerebral hemisphere

Right cerebral hemisphere

Frontal lobe

Cerebral artery

Parietal lobe

Cerebral vein

Superior sagittal sinus

Meninges (cut edge)

Occipital lobe

SUPERIOR VIEW OF BRAIN

FIRST AMERICAN EDITION, 1996
4 6 8 10 9 7 5 3

PUBLISHED IN THE UNITED STATES BY DK PUBLISHING, INC., 95 MADISON AVENUE, NEW YORK, NY 10016
FIRST PUBLISHED IN GREAT BRITAIN IN 1996 BY DORLING KINDERSLEY LIMITED, 9 HENRIETTA STREET, LONDON WC2E 8PS

COPYRIGHT © 1996 DORLING KINDERSLEY LIMITED, LONDON
TEXT COPYRIGHT © 1996 RICHARD WALKER
VISIT US ON THE WORLD WIDE WEB AT
HTTP://WWW.DK.COM

ISBN 0-7894-0445-1

LC NUMBER 95-52789
A CATALOG RECORD IS AVAILABLE FROM THE LIBRARY OF CONGRESS.

REPRODUCED BY COLOURSCAN, SINGAPORE.
PRINTED AND BOUND BY ARNOLDO MONDADORI, VERONA, ITALY.

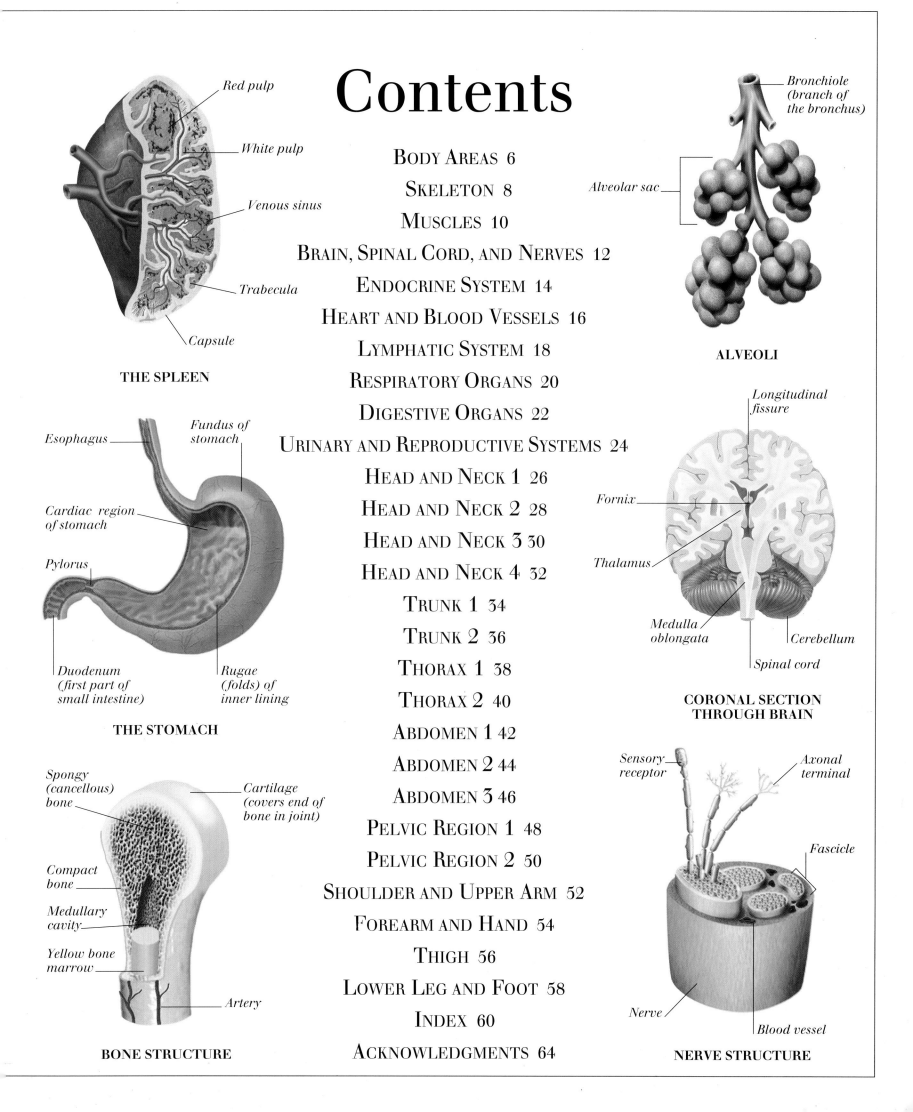

Contents

Red pulp

White pulp

Venous sinus

Trabecula

Capsule

THE SPLEEN

Esophagus

Fundus of stomach

Cardiac region of stomach

Pylorus

Duodenum (first part of small intestine)

Rugae (folds) of inner lining

THE STOMACH

Spongy (cancellous) bone

Cartilage (covers end of bone in joint)

Compact bone

Medullary cavity

Yellow bone marrow

Artery

BONE STRUCTURE

Bronchiole (branch of the bronchus)

Alveolar sac

ALVEOLI

Longitudinal fissure

Fornix

Thalamus

Medulla oblongata

Cerebellum

Spinal cord

CORONAL SECTION THROUGH BRAIN

Sensory receptor

Axonal terminal

Fascicle

Nerve

Blood vessel

NERVE STRUCTURE

Body areas

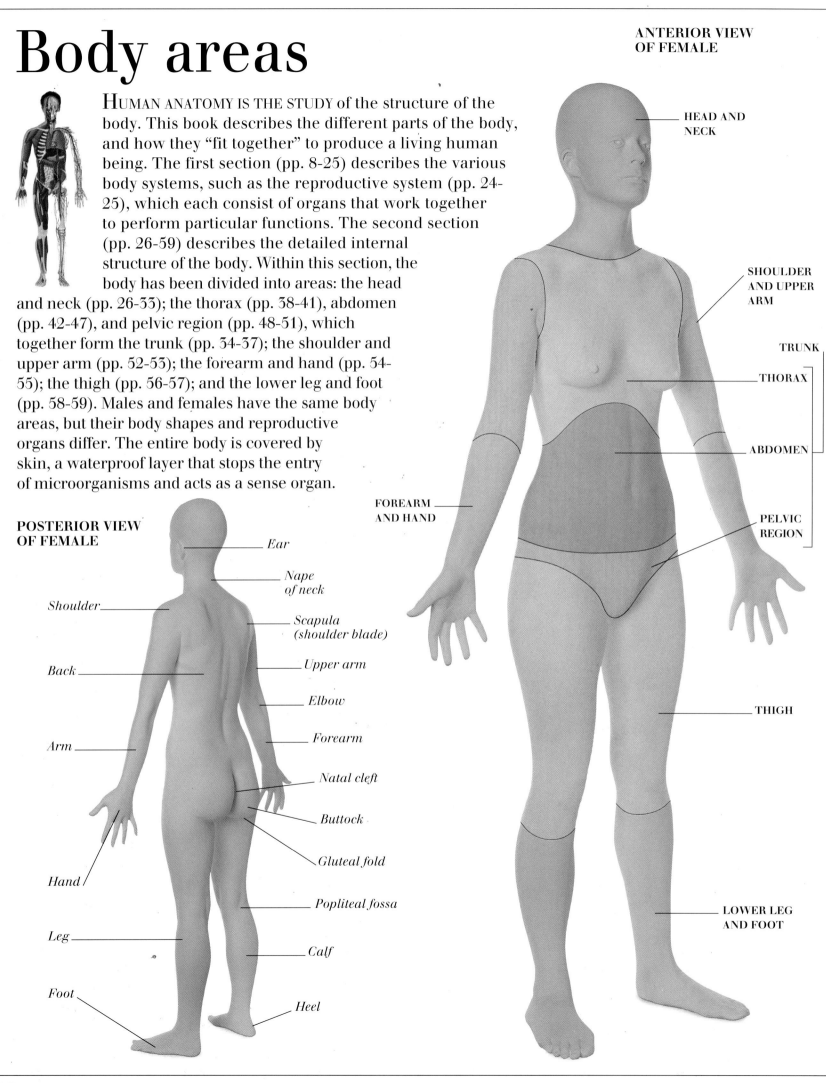

HUMAN ANATOMY IS THE STUDY of the structure of the body. This book describes the different parts of the body, and how they "fit together" to produce a living human being. The first section (pp. 8-25) describes the various body systems, such as the reproductive system (pp. 24-25), which each consist of organs that work together to perform particular functions. The second section (pp. 26-59) describes the detailed internal structure of the body. Within this section, the body has been divided into areas: the head and neck (pp. 26-33); the thorax (pp. 38-41), abdomen (pp. 42-47), and pelvic region (pp. 48-51), which together form the trunk (pp. 34-37); the shoulder and upper arm (pp. 52-53); the forearm and hand (pp. 54-55); the thigh (pp. 56-57); and the lower leg and foot (pp. 58-59). Males and females have the same body areas, but their body shapes and reproductive organs differ. The entire body is covered by skin, a waterproof layer that stops the entry of microorganisms and acts as a sense organ.

ANTERIOR VIEW OF FEMALE

HEAD AND NECK

SHOULDER AND UPPER ARM

TRUNK

THORAX

ABDOMEN

FOREARM AND HAND

PELVIC REGION

THIGH

LOWER LEG AND FOOT

POSTERIOR VIEW OF FEMALE

Ear

Nape of neck

Shoulder

Scapula (shoulder blade)

Back

Upper arm

Elbow

Arm

Forearm

Natal cleft

Buttock

Gluteal fold

Hand

Popliteal fossa

Leg

Calf

Foot

Heel

ANTERIOR VIEW OF MALE

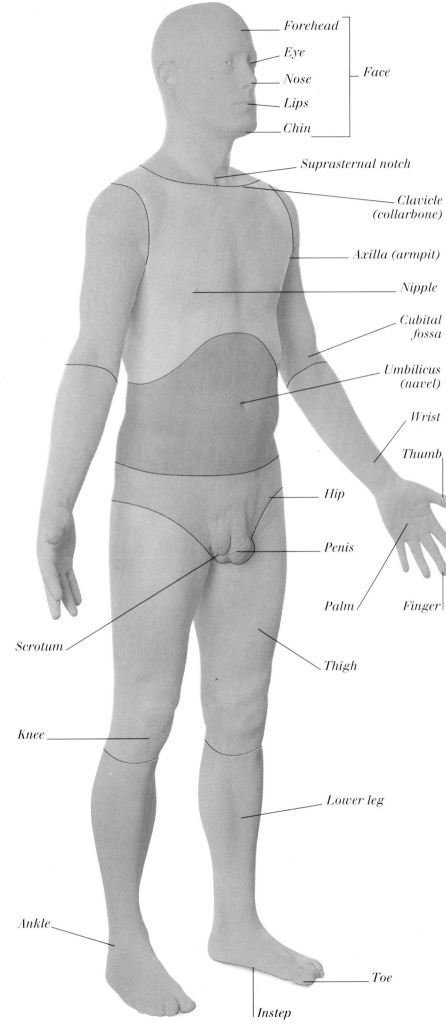

- Forehead
- Eye
- Nose — Face
- Lips
- Chin
- Suprasternal notch
- Clavicle (collarbone)
- Axilla (armpit)
- Nipple
- Cubital fossa
- Umbilicus (navel)
- Wrist
- Thumb
- Hip
- Penis
- Palm
- Finger
- Scrotum
- Thigh
- Knee
- Lower leg
- Ankle
- Toe
- Instep

SKIN, HAIR, AND NAILS

DERMIS
Skin consists of two layers, the outer epidermis and the dermis. The dermis contains nerve endings, hair follicles, and oil-producing sebaceous glands.

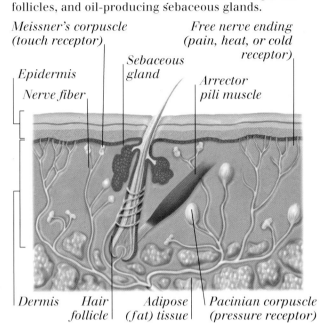

- Meissner's corpuscle (touch receptor)
- Free nerve ending (pain, heat, or cold receptor)
- Sebaceous gland
- Epidermis
- Arrector pili muscle
- Nerve fiber
- Dermis
- Hair follicle
- Adipose (fat) tissue
- Pacinian corpuscle (pressure receptor)

EPIDERMIS
The uppermost of the five epidermal layers consists of tough, flattened cell remnants that protect the lower layers. The upper layer is continually worn away and replaced by cells produced by the basal layer; these flatten and die as they move toward the surface.

- Stratum corneum (cornified layer)
- Stratum lucidum (clear layer)
- Stratum granulosum (granular layer)
- Stratum spinosum (prickly layer)
- Stratum basale (basal layer)
- Epidermal cell

NAIL STRUCTURE
Nails are plates that are derived from the epidermis. They contain keratin to make them hard. Their function is to protect the tips of the fingers and toes and to help the fingers grasp small objects. Nail grows from the matrix, where nail cells divide, lengthening the nail plate by pushing it forward over the nail bed.

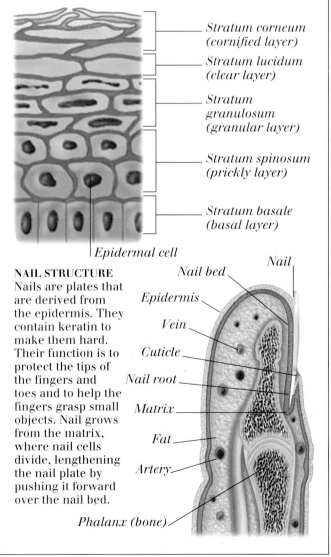

- Nail
- Nail bed
- Epidermis
- Vein
- Cuticle
- Nail root
- Matrix
- Fat
- Artery
- Phalanx (bone)

Skeleton

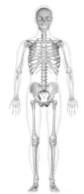

THE SKELETON IS A STRONG but lightweight framework that supports the body, protects the major organs, and enables movement to take place. In adults, it consists of 206 bones, and makes up 20 percent of the body's mass. Bone is a living tissue, supplied by blood vessels and nerves. In addition to its supportive role, it also stores calcium and other minerals, and manufactures blood cells.

The skeleton is divided into two parts. The axial skeleton forms the axis of the body trunk and consists of the skull, which protects the brain; the vertebral column, which surrounds the spinal cord; and the ribs, which encircle the heart and lungs, and assist in breathing. The appendicular skeleton consists of the bones of the arms and legs, as well as those of the pectoral (shoulder) and pelvic (hip) girdles that attach the limbs to the axial skeleton. Where two or more bones meet, a joint is formed. Joints are held together and stabilized by tough, straplike ligaments. Muscles attached to the bones on both sides of a joint produce movement when they contract.

BONES OF THE BODY

There are four basic types of bones that make up the body's internal framework: long bones, such as the femur and humerus; flat bones, such as the ribs and most skull bones; short bones, such as the carpals and tarsals; and irregular bones, such as the vertebrae.

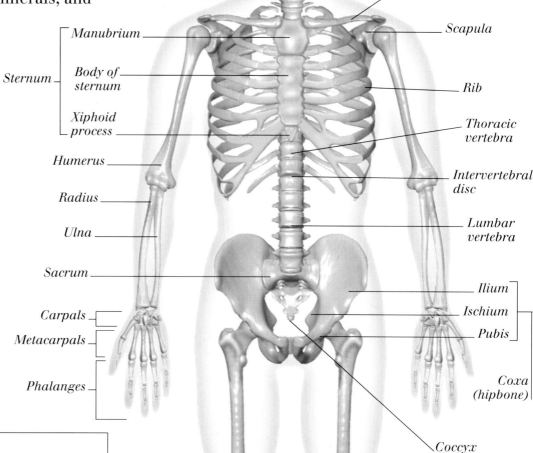

Skull

Mandible

Cervical vertebra

Clavicle

Scapula

Manubrium

Sternum

Body of sternum

Rib

Xiphoid process

Thoracic vertebra

Humerus

Intervertebral disc

Radius

Lumbar vertebra

Ulna

Sacrum

Ilium

Carpals

Ischium

Metacarpals

Pubis

Phalanges

Coxa (hipbone)

Coccyx

Femur

Patella

Tibia

Fibula

Tarsals
Metatarsals
Phalanges

BONE STRUCTURE

The combination of an outer covering of dense compact bone with an inner layer of lighter, spongy bone makes bones both strong and light. A medullary canal, which contains marrow, runs along the length of the shaft of long bones.

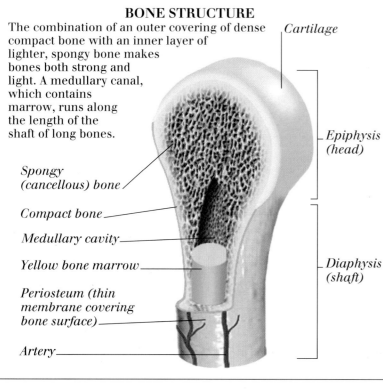

Cartilage

Epiphysis (head)

Spongy (cancellous) bone

Compact bone

Medullary cavity

Yellow bone marrow

Diaphysis (shaft)

Periosteum (thin membrane covering bone surface)

Artery

EXPLODED LATERAL VIEW OF THE SKULL

The skull surrounds and protects the brain and forms the framework of the face. It consists of 22 bones. Apart from the freely movable mandible (lower jaw), these bones are united by immovable interlocking joints called sutures.

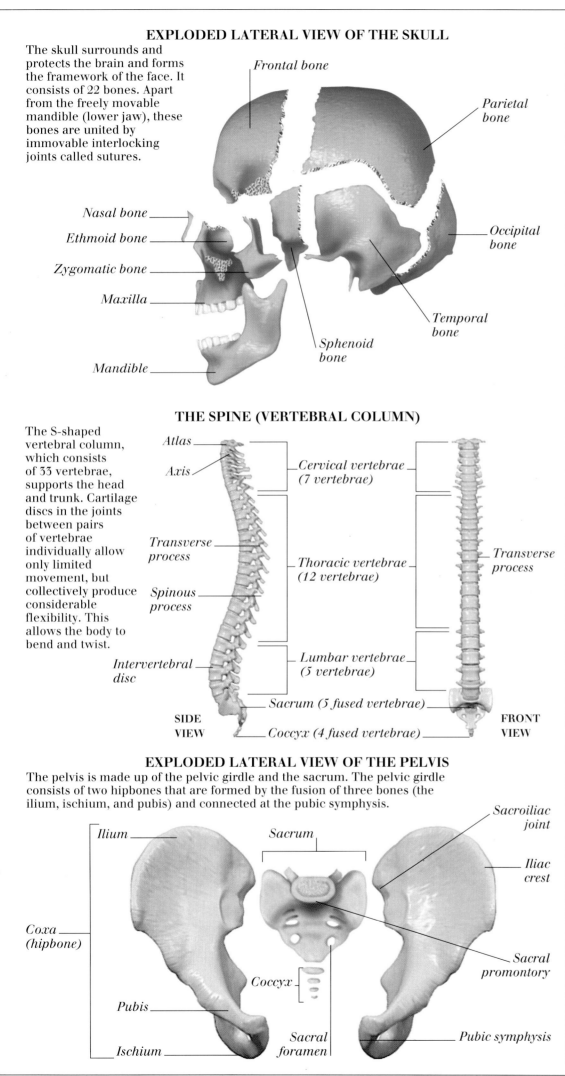

Frontal bone

Parietal bone

Nasal bone

Ethmoid bone

Zygomatic bone

Maxilla

Mandible

Occipital bone

Temporal bone

Sphenoid bone

THE SPINE (VERTEBRAL COLUMN)

The S-shaped vertebral column, which consists of 33 vertebrae, supports the head and trunk. Cartilage discs in the joints between pairs of vertebrae individually allow only limited movement, but collectively produce considerable flexibility. This allows the body to bend and twist.

Atlas

Axis

Transverse process

Spinous process

Intervertebral disc

Cervical vertebrae (7 vertebrae)

Thoracic vertebrae (12 vertebrae)

Lumbar vertebrae (5 vertebrae)

Sacrum (5 fused vertebrae)

Coccyx (4 fused vertebrae)

Transverse process

SIDE VIEW

FRONT VIEW

EXPLODED LATERAL VIEW OF THE PELVIS

The pelvis is made up of the pelvic girdle and the sacrum. The pelvic girdle consists of two hipbones that are formed by the fusion of three bones (the ilium, ischium, and pubis) and connected at the pubic symphysis.

Ilium

Sacrum

Sacroiliac joint

Iliac crest

Coxa (hipbone)

Coccyx

Sacral promontory

Pubis

Ischium

Sacral foramen

Pubic symphysis

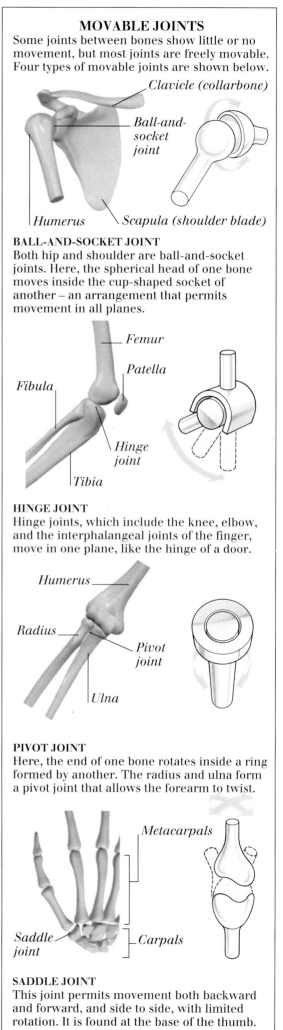

MOVABLE JOINTS
Some joints between bones show little or no movement, but most joints are freely movable. Four types of movable joints are shown below.

Clavicle (collarbone)

Ball-and-socket joint

Humerus

Scapula (shoulder blade)

BALL-AND-SOCKET JOINT
Both hip and shoulder are ball-and-socket joints. Here, the spherical head of one bone moves inside the cup-shaped socket of another – an arrangement that permits movement in all planes.

Femur

Patella

Fibula

Hinge joint

Tibia

HINGE JOINT
Hinge joints, which include the knee, elbow, and the interphalangeal joints of the finger, move in one plane, like the hinge of a door.

Humerus

Radius

Pivot joint

Ulna

PIVOT JOINT
Here, the end of one bone rotates inside a ring formed by another. The radius and ulna form a pivot joint that allows the forearm to twist.

Metacarpals

Saddle joint

Carpals

SADDLE JOINT
This joint permits movement both backward and forward, and side to side, with limited rotation. It is found at the base of the thumb.

Muscles

MUSCLE IS TISSUE that can contract, or shorten, in response to a nerve impulse (message) from the central nervous system (the brain and spinal cord). Three types of muscle – skeletal, smooth, and cardiac – make up nearly 40 percent of the body's weight. Over 600 skeletal, or voluntary, muscles operate under conscious control to move the body, stabilize joints, and maintain body posture. Skeletal muscles are attached to bones by tough, fibrous cords called tendons. Typically, each muscle connects two bones by stretching across the joint between them. When the muscle contracts, one bone (the muscle's origin) remains fixed in position, while the other (the muscle's insertion) moves. Muscles lying near the skin's surface are called superficial, while those layered beneath them are called deep. Smooth, or involuntary, muscle is found in the walls of hollow organs, such as the intestine, and performs functions that are not under conscious control, such as moving partially digested food. Cardiac muscle is found only in the heart. It contracts rhythmically to pump blood around the body, but needs external nerve stimulation to accelerate or slow its pace.

TENDON

A tendon links a muscle to a bone. Tendons consist of strong connective tissue packed with tough collagen fibers. When a muscle contracts, the tendon pulls the bone, causing it to move. Most tendons are cordlike, but some, known as aponeuroses, are broad and flat.

Epimysium (layer of tissue covering muscle)

Muscle

Tendon

Bone

Periosteum (layer of tissue covering bone)

NEUROMUSCULAR JUNCTION

Skeletal muscle fibers (cells) contract when stimulated by nerve impulses arriving along a motor neuron (nerve cell). A neuromuscular (nerve–muscle) junction is the site at which motor neuron and muscle fiber meet but do not touch; there is a tiny gap, or synapse, between them, across which impulses are transmitted chemically.

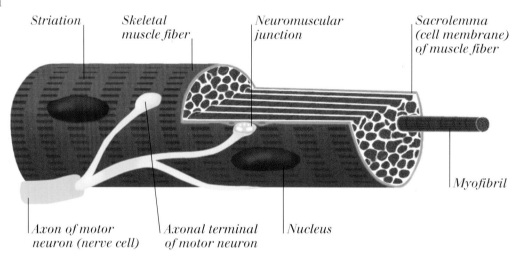

Striation

Skeletal muscle fiber

Neuromuscular junction

Sacrolemma (cell membrane) of muscle fiber

Myofibril

Axon of motor neuron (nerve cell)

Axonal terminal of motor neuron

Nucleus

TYPES OF MUSCLE

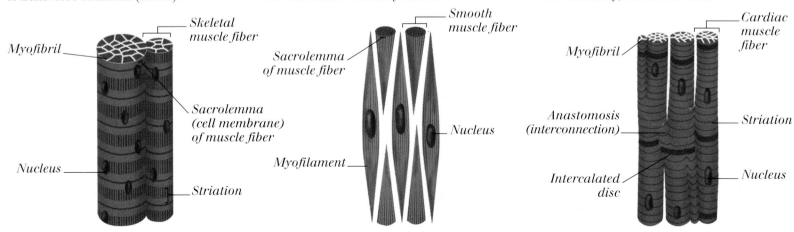

SKELETAL MUSCLE

Skeletal muscle makes up the bulk of the body's muscles. It consists of long, cylindrical muscle fibers (cells), which lie parallel to each other. Each fiber has a regular pattern of transverse striations (bands).

Myofibril

Skeletal muscle fiber

Sacrolemma (cell membrane) of muscle fiber

Nucleus

Striation

SMOOTH MUSCLE

Smooth muscle, found in the walls of internal organs, consists of short, spindle-shaped muscle fibers (cells) packed together in muscle sheets. Its slow, sustained contractions are not under voluntary control.

Smooth muscle fiber

Sacrolemma of muscle fiber

Nucleus

Myofilament

CARDIAC MUSCLE

Cardiac muscle, contained in the heart wall, consists of anastomosing (branched) chains of muscle fibers (cells) which, like skeletal fibers, are striated. It relaxes and contracts automatically, and never tires.

Cardiac muscle fiber

Myofibril

Anastomosis (interconnection)

Striation

Intercalated disc

Nucleus

MAJOR SKELETAL MUSCLES

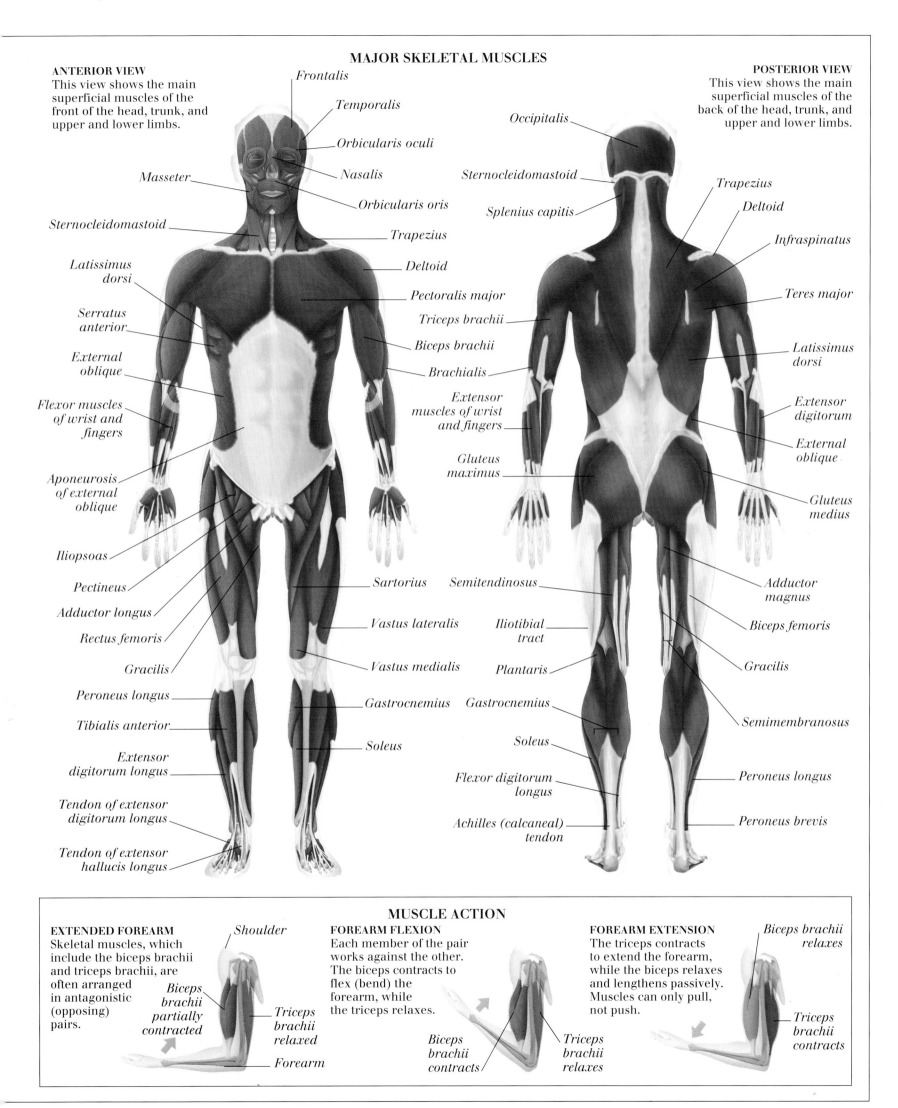

ANTERIOR VIEW
This view shows the main superficial muscles of the front of the head, trunk, and upper and lower limbs.

POSTERIOR VIEW
This view shows the main superficial muscles of the back of the head, trunk, and upper and lower limbs.

Frontalis

Temporalis

Orbicularis oculi

Nasalis

Orbicularis oris

Masseter

Sternocleidomastoid

Latissimus dorsi

Serratus anterior

External oblique

Flexor muscles of wrist and fingers

Aponeurosis of external oblique

Iliopsoas

Pectineus

Adductor longus

Rectus femoris

Gracilis

Peroneus longus

Tibialis anterior

Extensor digitorum longus

Tendon of extensor digitorum longus

Tendon of extensor hallucis longus

Trapezius

Deltoid

Pectoralis major

Triceps brachii

Biceps brachii

Brachialis

Extensor muscles of wrist and fingers

Gluteus maximus

Sartorius

Vastus lateralis

Vastus medialis

Gastrocnemius

Soleus

Occipitalis

Sternocleidomastoid

Splenius capitis

Trapezius

Deltoid

Infraspinatus

Teres major

Latissimus dorsi

Extensor digitorum

External oblique

Gluteus medius

Semitendinosus

Iliotibial tract

Plantaris

Gastrocnemius

Soleus

Flexor digitorum longus

Achilles (calcaneal) tendon

Adductor magnus

Biceps femoris

Gracilis

Semimembranosus

Peroneus longus

Peroneus brevis

MUSCLE ACTION

EXTENDED FOREARM
Skeletal muscles, which include the biceps brachii and triceps brachii, are often arranged in antagonistic (opposing) pairs.

Shoulder

Biceps brachii partially contracted

Triceps brachii relaxed

Forearm

FOREARM FLEXION
Each member of the pair works against the other. The biceps contracts to flex (bend) the forearm, while the triceps relaxes.

Biceps brachii contracts

Triceps brachii relaxes

FOREARM EXTENSION
The triceps contracts to extend the forearm, while the biceps relaxes and lengthens passively. Muscles can only pull, not push.

Biceps brachii relaxes

Triceps brachii contracts

Brain, spinal cord, and nerves

THE BRAIN, SPINAL CORD, AND NERVES together form the nervous system, the communication network of the body. It has two main parts: the central nervous system (CNS), which consists of the brain and spinal cord, and is the control center of the network; and the peripheral nervous system (PNS) which consists of cablelike nerves that link the CNS to the rest of the body. The nervous system contains billions of intercommunicating neurons, highly specialized cells capable of rapidly transmitting impulses (one-way electrochemical messages). There are three types of neurons. Sensory neurons, the first, carry impulses from internal and external sensory receptors, such as the eye and ear, to the CNS, constantly updating it about events occurring both inside and outside the body. Motor neurons, the second type, transmit impulses from the CNS to effector organs, such as muscles, instructing them to respond by contracting. Sensory and motor neurons are bundled together to form nerves. Association neurons, the third type, are found only in the CNS, and link sensory and motor neurons. They form complex pathways that enable the brain to interpret incoming sensory messages, compare them with past experiences, decide on what should be done, and, in response, send out instructions along motor pathways to keep the body functioning properly.

THE NERVE NETWORK

Twelve pairs of cranial nerves arising from the brain, and 31 pairs of spinal nerves arising from the spinal cord connect the brain and spinal cord to all parts of the body.

Cerebrum

Cranial nerve

Cervical nerves (8 pairs)

Brachial plexus

Musculocutaneous nerve

Axillary nerve

Thoracic nerves (12 pairs)

Spinal cord

Radial nerve

Median nerve

Ulnar nerve

Lumbar nerves (5 pairs)

Lumbar plexus

Sacral plexus

Sacral nerves (5 pairs)

Femoral nerve

Median nerve

Radial nerve

Ulnar nerve

Sciatic nerve

Coccygeal nerve

Common peroneal nerve

Tibial nerve

Medial plantar nerve

Saphenous nerve

Lateral plantar nerve

ANATOMY OF THE SPINAL CORD

The spinal cord forms a two-way information pathway between the brain and the rest of the body via the spinal nerves. It is protected by three layers of tissue called meninges and by cerebrospinal fluid circulating in the subarachnoid space.

Gray matter

Central canal

Meninges

Dorsal root

White matter

Ventral root

Pia mater

Spinal nerve

Arachnoid

Anterior median fissure

Dura mater

THE BRAIN

The brain, with the spinal cord, controls and coordinates all body functions. The largest part of the brain is the cerebrum, which is divided into two halves, the left and right cerebral hemispheres. The outer, thin layer of the cerebrum (the cerebral cortex) consists of gray matter (the cell bodies of neurons); the inner part is white matter (nerve fibers). The cerebral cortex is the site of conscious behavior. Different areas of the cortex are responsible for different functions such as movement, touch, vision, hearing, and thought. The cerebellum, the second largest part of the brain, coordinates balance and movement. The brain stem (the midbrain, pons, and medulla oblongata) regulates heartbeat, breathing, and other vital functions. The thalamus relays and sorts the nerve impulses that pass between the spinal cord and brain stem, and the cerebrum.

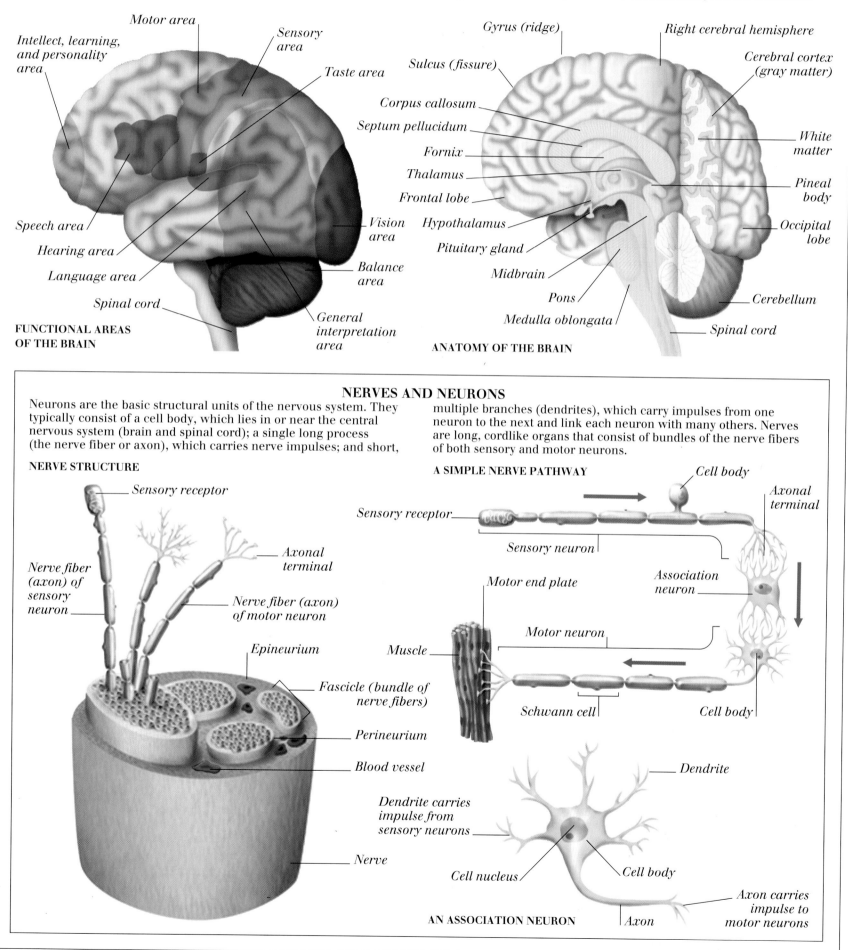

Motor area

Sensory area

Intellect, learning, and personality area

Taste area

Speech area

Hearing area

Language area

Spinal cord

Vision area

Balance area

General interpretation area

FUNCTIONAL AREAS OF THE BRAIN

Gyrus (ridge)

Right cerebral hemisphere

Sulcus (fissure)

Cerebral cortex (gray matter)

Corpus callosum

Septum pellucidum

Fornix

Thalamus

Frontal lobe

Hypothalamus

Pituitary gland

Midbrain

Pons

Medulla oblongata

White matter

Pineal body

Occipital lobe

Cerebellum

Spinal cord

ANATOMY OF THE BRAIN

NERVES AND NEURONS

Neurons are the basic structural units of the nervous system. They typically consist of a cell body, which lies in or near the central nervous system (brain and spinal cord); a single long process (the nerve fiber or axon), which carries nerve impulses; and short, multiple branches (dendrites), which carry impulses from one neuron to the next and link each neuron with many others. Nerves are long, cordlike organs that consist of bundles of the nerve fibers of both sensory and motor neurons.

NERVE STRUCTURE

Sensory receptor

Nerve fiber (axon) of sensory neuron

Axonal terminal

Nerve fiber (axon) of motor neuron

Epineurium

Fascicle (bundle of nerve fibers)

Perineurium

Blood vessel

Nerve

A SIMPLE NERVE PATHWAY

Cell body

Axonal terminal

Sensory receptor

Sensory neuron

Association neuron

Motor end plate

Motor neuron

Muscle

Schwann cell

Cell body

Dendrite

Dendrite carries impulse from sensory neurons

Cell nucleus

Cell body

AN ASSOCIATION NEURON

Axon

Axon carries impulse to motor neurons

Endocrine system

THE ENDOCRINE, OR HORMONAL, SYSTEM consists of a number of endocrine glands, which are scattered around the body. These glands manufacture chemical messengers called hormones, and release them into the bloodstream. Hormones control the rate at which specific target organs or glands work. Together, the endocrine system and the nervous system (see pp. 12–13) control and coordinate all the body's activities. While the nervous system acts rapidly, with short-lived results, hormones act more slowly, and with longer-lasting effects. The endocrine glands include the pineal, which controls the daily rhythms of sleeping and waking; the parathyroids, which determine calcium levels in the blood; the thyroid, which controls metabolism (the rate at which the body uses energy); the adrenals, which release a number of hormones, including fast-acting epinephrine, which increases the heart rate under stress conditions; the pancreas, which controls the level of blood glucose (the body's energy supply); and the ovaries and testes, which release the sex hormones that produce secondary sexual characteristics, such as breasts in women and facial hair in men. Most, but not all, endocrine glands are controlled by hormones released by the pituitary gland in the brain. This, in turn, is controlled by the hypothalamus – an adjacent part of the brain.

ENDOCRINE GLANDS OF THE BRAIN
The hypothalamus plays an important part in coordinating hormone production. It sends instructions to the nearby pituitary gland, which then releases hormones that target other endocrine glands.

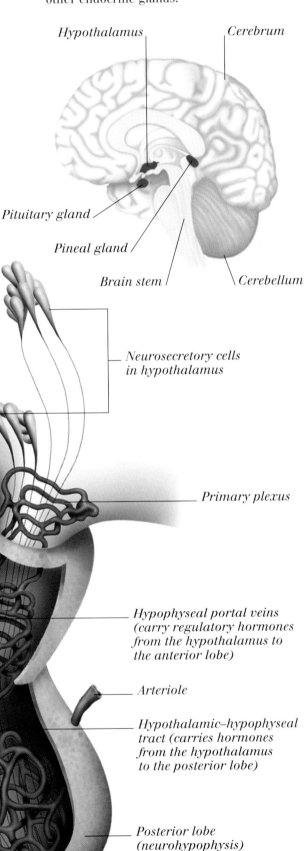

Hypothalamus

Cerebrum

Pituitary gland

Pineal gland

Brain stem

Cerebellum

Neurosecretory cells in hypothalamus

Primary plexus

THE PITUITARY GLAND
The pituitary consists of two parts. The anterior lobe produces a number of hormones, including growth hormone and thyroid-stimulating hormone, which stimulates the thyroid gland to release hormones. The posterior lobe stores two hormones produced by the hypothalamus: oxytocin, which causes uterine contractions during labor, and antidiuretic hormone, which controls urine concentration.

Infundibulum (pituitary stalk)

Hypophyseal portal veins (carry regulatory hormones from the hypothalamus to the anterior lobe)

Arteriole

Hypothalamic–hypophyseal tract (carries hormones from the hypothalamus to the posterior lobe)

Secondary plexus

Posterior lobe (neurohypophysis)

Anterior lobe (adenohypophysis)

Secretory cells of anterior lobe

Venules

HOW THE ENDOCRINE SYSTEM WORKS

Hormones manufactured by an endocrine gland are secreted into the circulatory system and carried in the blood to specific target tissues. Here, they attach themselves to tissue cells and exert their effect.

THE RELEASE OF HORMONES INTO THE BLOODSTREAM

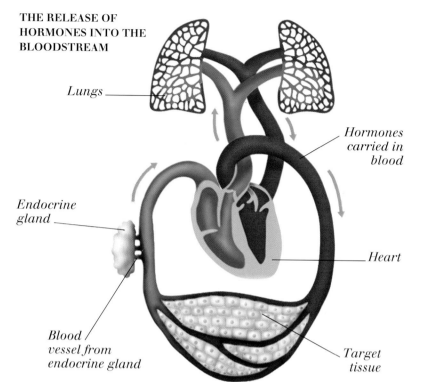

Lungs

Hormones carried in blood

Endocrine gland

Heart

Blood vessel from endocrine gland

Target tissue

ENDOCRINE GLANDS

Even though they are scattered around the body, most of the endocrine glands come under the control of the pituitary gland.

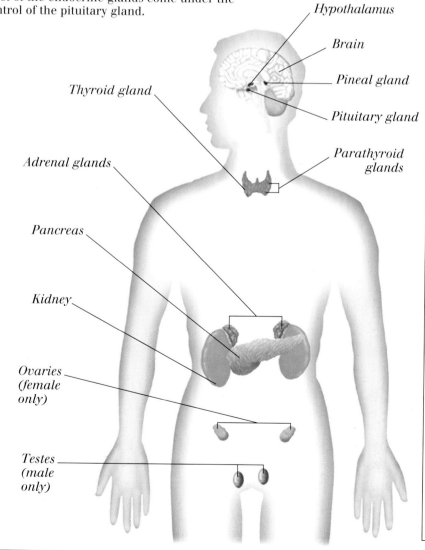

Hypothalamus

Brain

Pineal gland

Thyroid gland

Pituitary gland

Adrenal glands

Parathyroid glands

Pancreas

Kidney

Ovaries (female only)

Testes (male only)

HORMONE-PRODUCING GLANDS

The hormone-producing endocrine glands are also known as ductless glands. Unlike other glands, such as salivary glands, which release their products along ducts, endocrine glands release their products directly into the bloodstream.

POSTERIOR VIEW OF THE THYROID GLAND

The thyroid gland produces two hormones: thyroxine, which speeds up metabolism, and calcitonin, which decreases calcium levels in the blood. The parathyroids produce parathyroid hormone, which increases blood calcium levels.

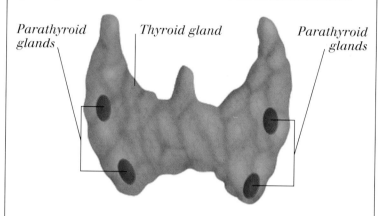

Parathyroid glands

Thyroid gland

Parathyroid glands

THE PANCREAS

The pancreas produces two hormones, insulin and glucagon, which respectively decrease and increase the level of blood glucose to keep it within set limits. The pancreas also has an exocrine (ducted) portion that produces digestive enzymes.

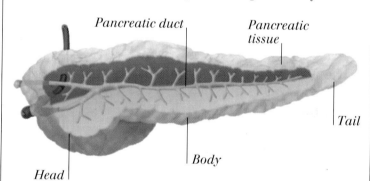

Pancreatic duct

Pancreatic tissue

Head

Body

Tail

ADRENAL GLANDS

On top of each kidney there is an adrenal gland. The outer part (cortex) produces corticosteroids, which regulate blood concentration and influence metabolism. The inner part (medulla) produces epinephrine, which prepares the body for dealing with stress or danger by increasing heart and breathing rates.

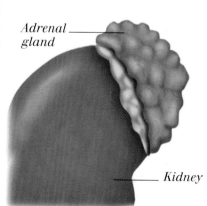

Adrenal gland

Kidney

OVARIES AND TESTES

Testes release testosterone, which controls sperm production. Ovaries release progesterone and estrogen, which prepare women's bodies for pregnancy. Secondary sexual characteristics such as facial hair and breasts are also produced by these hormones.

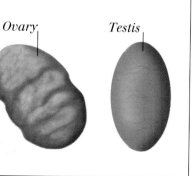

Ovary

Testis

Heart and blood vessels

THE HEART AND BLOOD VESSELS, together with the blood they contain, form the cardiovascular, or circulatory, system. This transports nutrients and oxygen to all body cells and removes their waste products. It also carries specialized cells that help protect against infection. The heart is a powerful muscle. It pumps blood around the circuit of blood vessels that supplies the whole body.

There are two circulatory routes: the pulmonary circulation, which carries blood through the lungs, and the systemic circulation, which carries blood through body tissues. The heart is composed of two halves, each divided into an atrium (upper chamber) and a ventricle (lower chamber). Blood returning from the body to the heart is low in oxygen. It enters the right atrium, passes into the right ventricle, and is pumped into the lungs, where it is enriched with oxygen. The oxygen-rich blood passes back into the left atrium and is pumped back into the body via the left ventricle.

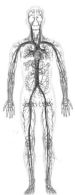

THE CIRCULATORY SYSTEM
This consists of a massive network of over 60,000 miles (100,000 km) of blood vessels (arteries, veins, and capillaries). This circulates blood between the heart and all parts of the body.

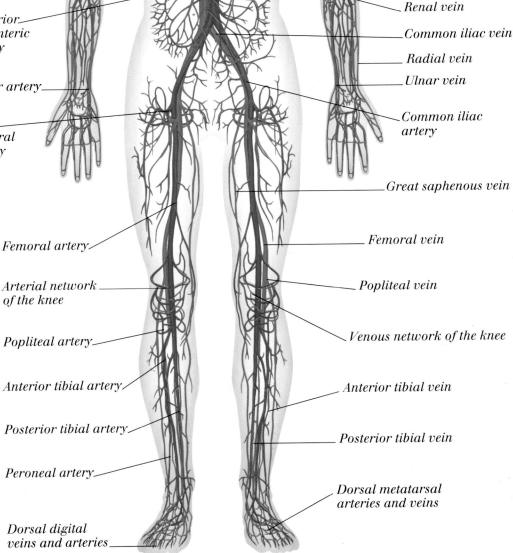

Common carotid artery

Subclavian artery

Superior vena cava

Pulmonary artery

Axillary artery

Pulmonary vein

Brachial artery

Inferior vena cava

Hepatic portal vein

Superior mesenteric artery

Ulnar artery

Deep femoral artery

Internal jugular vein

Subclavian vein

Aortic arch

Heart

Axillary vein

Cephalic vein

Brachial vein

Basilic vein

Descending aorta

Renal artery

Renal vein

Common iliac vein

Radial vein

Ulnar vein

Common iliac artery

Great saphenous vein

Femoral artery

Femoral vein

Arterial network of the knee

Popliteal vein

Popliteal artery

Venous network of the knee

Anterior tibial artery

Anterior tibial vein

Posterior tibial artery

Posterior tibial vein

Peroneal artery

Dorsal metatarsal arteries and veins

Dorsal digital veins and arteries

BLOOD VESSELS
Thick-walled arteries carry blood at high pressure. They branch repeatedly to form microscopic capillaries that carry blood through the tissues, and then merge to form veins that carry blood back to the heart.

ARTERY　　　**VEIN**

Endothelium

Lumen

Middle layer of smooth muscle

Lumen

Endothelium

CAPILLARY

THE HEART

The heart is made of cardiac muscle that contracts automatically and never tires. The left pump pushes blood around the body; the right pump pushes blood into the lungs. Both sides beat together in a cycle with three stages: diastole, atrial systole, and ventricular systole.

ANTERIOR VIEW

- Superior vena cava
- Aortic arch
- Aortic semilunar valve
- Pulmonary trunk
- Right atrium
- Left atrium
- Right pulmonary veins
- Right ventricle
- Left ventricle
- Inferior vena cava
- Right ventricle

INTERIOR VIEW

- Left common carotid artery
- Brachiocephalic artery
- Aortic arch
- Left subclavian artery
- Left pulmonary artery
- Pulmonary semilunar valve
- Right atrium
- Tricuspid valve
- Left atrium
- Bicuspid (mitral) valve
- Right ventricle
- Septum
- Left ventricle

DIASTOLE
Blood returning from the body flows into the right atrium, and oxygen-rich blood flowing from the lungs flows into the left atrium.

- Right and left atria relaxed
- Tricuspid valve opens
- Ventricles relaxed

ATRIAL SYSTOLE
The right and left atria contract to push blood into the ventricles. The semilunar valves close to stop blood from flowing back into the heart.

- Atria contract
- Bicuspid (mitral) valve opens
- Ventricles relaxed
- Tricuspid valve closes

VENTRICULAR SYSTOLE
The ventricles contract to push blood out of the heart through semilunar valves. The bicuspid and tricuspid valves close to prevent backflow.

- Semilunar valves open
- Bicuspid (mitral) valve closes
- Ventricles contract

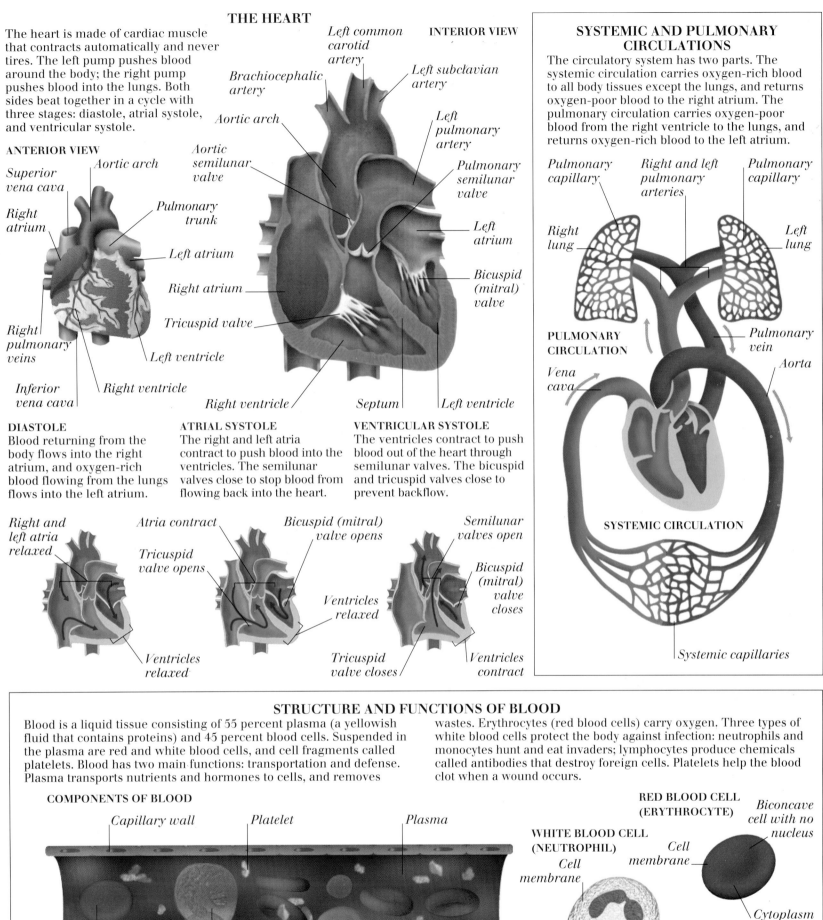

SYSTEMIC AND PULMONARY CIRCULATIONS

The circulatory system has two parts. The systemic circulation carries oxygen-rich blood to all body tissues except the lungs, and returns oxygen-poor blood to the right atrium. The pulmonary circulation carries oxygen-poor blood from the right ventricle to the lungs, and returns oxygen-rich blood to the left atrium.

- Pulmonary capillary
- Right and left pulmonary arteries
- Pulmonary capillary
- Right lung
- Left lung
- **PULMONARY CIRCULATION**
- Pulmonary vein
- Vena cava
- Aorta
- **SYSTEMIC CIRCULATION**
- Systemic capillaries

STRUCTURE AND FUNCTIONS OF BLOOD

Blood is a liquid tissue consisting of 55 percent plasma (a yellowish fluid that contains proteins) and 45 percent blood cells. Suspended in the plasma are red and white blood cells, and cell fragments called platelets. Blood has two main functions: transportation and defense. Plasma transports nutrients and hormones to cells, and removes wastes. Erythrocytes (red blood cells) carry oxygen. Three types of white blood cells protect the body against infection: neutrophils and monocytes hunt and eat invaders; lymphocytes produce chemicals called antibodies that destroy foreign cells. Platelets help the blood clot when a wound occurs.

COMPONENTS OF BLOOD

- Capillary wall
- Platelet
- Plasma
- Erythrocyte (red blood cell)
- Neutrophil (white blood cell)
- Lymphocyte (white blood cell)

WHITE BLOOD CELL (NEUTROPHIL)

- Cell membrane
- Granular cytoplasm
- Multilobed nucleus

RED BLOOD CELL (ERYTHROCYTE)

- Biconcave cell with no nucleus
- Cell membrane
- Cytoplasm filled with hemoglobin

- Cell fragment
- Granular cytoplasm
- **PLATELETS**

Lymphatic system

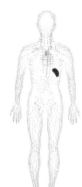

THE LYMPHATIC SYSTEM removes excess fluid from the body's tissues and returns it to the circulatory system. It also helps the body fight infection. It consists of lymphatic vessels, lymph nodes, and associated lymphoid organs, such as the spleen and tonsils. Lymph vessels form a network of tubes that reach all over the body. The smallest vessels – lymphatic capillaries – end blindly in the body's tissues. Here, they collect a liquid called lymph, which leaks out of blood capillaries and accumulates in the tissues. Once collected, lymph flows in one direction along progressively larger vessels: first, lymphatic vessels; second, lymphatic trunks; and, finally, the thoracic and right lymphatic ducts, which empty the lymph into the bloodstream. Lymph nodes are swellings along lymphatic vessels that defend the body against disease by filtering disease-causing microorganisms, such as bacteria, as lymph passes through them. There are two types of defensive cells in lymph nodes: macrophages, which engulf microorganisms, and lymphocytes, which release antibodies that target and destroy microorganisms. Lymphoid organs also contain defensive cells that destroy microorganisms found in blood or, in the case of the tonsils, air. Lymphoid organs do not filter lymph.

THE LYMPHATIC SYSTEM

Fluid lost from the blood is constantly accumulating in the body's tissues. The lymphatic network returns this excess fluid back into the bloodstream, and at the same time filters out disease-causing microorganisms.

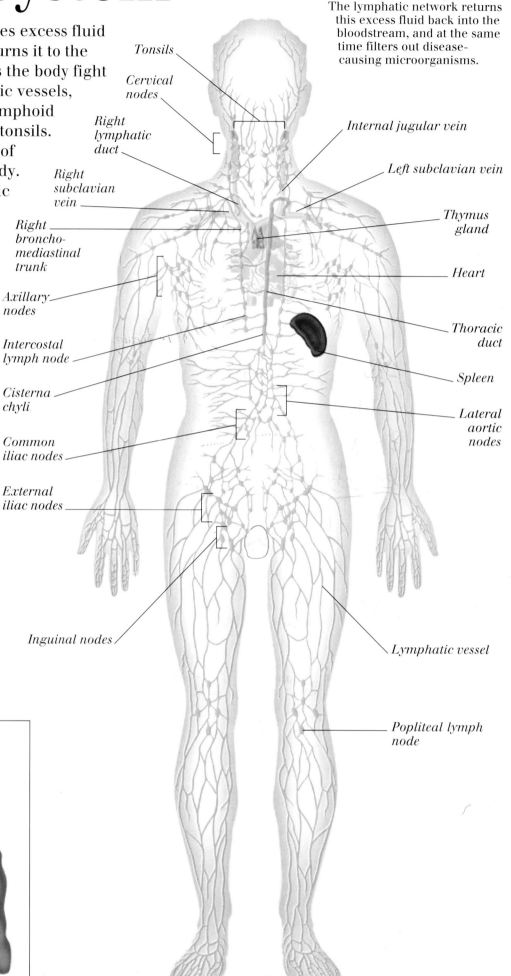

Tonsils

Cervical nodes

Right lymphatic duct

Right subclavian vein

Right broncho-mediastinal trunk

Axillary nodes

Intercostal lymph node

Cisterna chyli

Common iliac nodes

External iliac nodes

Inguinal nodes

Internal jugular vein

Left subclavian vein

Thymus gland

Heart

Thoracic duct

Spleen

Lateral aortic nodes

Lymphatic vessel

Popliteal lymph node

THE THYMUS GLAND

This lymphoid organ assists in the production of cells called "T lymphocytes," which target specific disease-causing micro-organisms for destruction and help defend the body against infection. The thymus is most active in children and gradually shrinks during adulthood.

Right lobe

Left lobe

HOW THE LYMPHATIC SYSTEM WORKS

Lymph capillaries join to form larger lymphatic vessels, which transport lymph and empty it into the bloodstream.

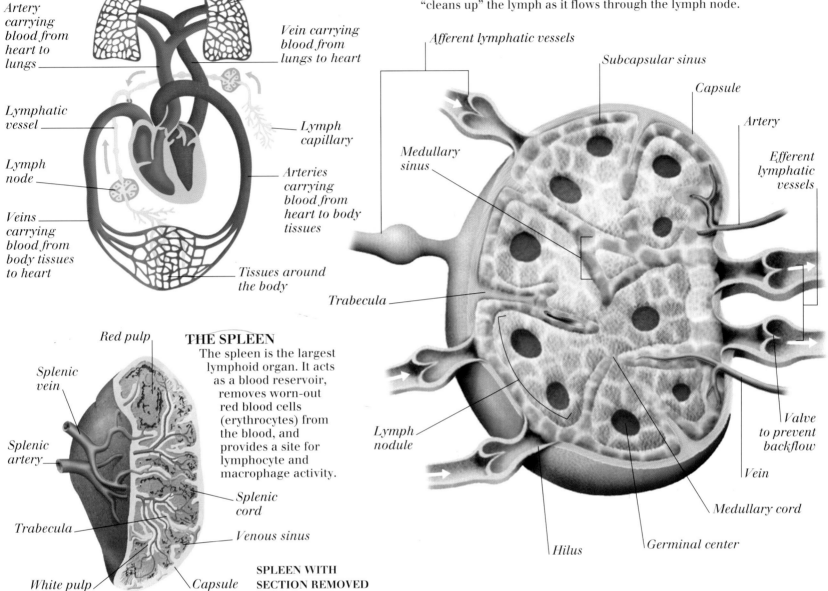

Artery carrying blood from heart to lungs

Lung

Vein carrying blood from lungs to heart

Lymphatic vessel

Lymph capillary

Lymph node

Arteries carrying blood from heart to body tissues

Veins carrying blood from body tissues to heart

Tissues around the body

THE SPLEEN

The spleen is the largest lymphoid organ. It acts as a blood reservoir, removes worn-out red blood cells (erythrocytes) from the blood, and provides a site for lymphocyte and macrophage activity.

Red pulp

Splenic vein

Splenic artery

Trabecula

White pulp

Splenic cord

Venous sinus

Capsule

SPLEEN WITH SECTION REMOVED

STRUCTURE OF A LYMPH NODE

Hundreds of these small, bean-shaped organs are clustered along lymphatic vessels. Each one is surrounded by a capsule and divided into compartments by trabeculae. These compartments contain a network of fibers supporting the lymphocytes and macrophages that filter out foreign microorganisms and general debris. This process "cleans up" the lymph as it flows through the lymph node.

Afferent lymphatic vessels

Subcapsular sinus

Capsule

Artery

Medullary sinus

Efferent lymphatic vessels

Trabecula

Valve to prevent backflow

Lymph nodule

Vein

Medullary cord

Hilus

Germinal center

ANTIBODY AND CELLULAR DEFENSES

The body has two mechanisms to protect itself from infection. The antibody defense system employs lymphocytes that release killer chemicals called antibodies. When substances called antigens – located on the surface of bacteria, viruses, and other disease-causing microorganisms – are detected, the antibodies target them and either disable or destroy them. The cellular defense system employs phagocytes ("cell eaters"), which seek out, engulf, and destroy invaders. Lymphocytes and phagocytes are found in both lymphatic and circulatory systems, and phagocytes also wander through the tissues. One type of phagocyte is called a macrophage.

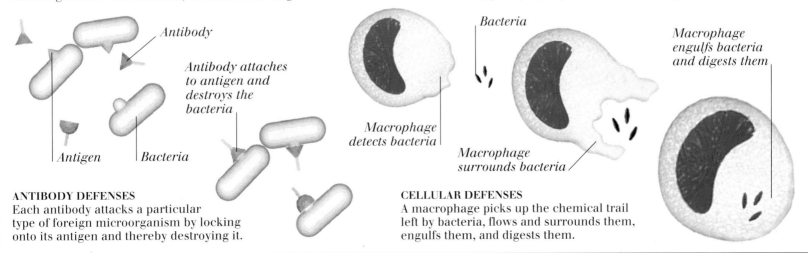

Antibody

Antibody attaches to antigen and destroys the bacteria

Antigen

Bacteria

Bacteria

Macrophage engulfs bacteria and digests them

Macrophage detects bacteria

Macrophage surrounds bacteria

ANTIBODY DEFENSES
Each antibody attacks a particular type of foreign microorganism by locking onto its antigen and thereby destroying it.

CELLULAR DEFENSES
A macrophage picks up the chemical trail left by bacteria, flows and surrounds them, engulfs them, and digests them.

Respiratory organs

THE RESPIRATORY ORGANS CONSIST OF THE NOSE, pharynx (throat), larynx (voice box), trachea (windpipe), the bronchi (sing. bronchus), and the lungs. Collectively, they form the respiratory system, which supplies the body with oxygen and removes waste carbon dioxide. Air is moved into and out of the respiratory system by breathing. During inhalation (breathing in), air is drawn in through the nose, pharynx, trachea, and bronchi, and into the lungs. Inside the lungs, each bronchus divides repeatedly to form a "tree" of tubes called bronchioles, which progressively decrease in diameter and end in microscopic air sacs called alveoli (sing. alveolus). Oxygen from the air that reaches the alveoli diffuses through the alveolar walls and into the surrounding blood capillaries. This oxygen-rich blood is carried first to the heart and is then pumped to cells throughout the body. Carbon dioxide diffuses out of the blood into the alveoli and is removed from the body during exhalation (breathing out). Breathing is the result of muscular contraction. During inhalation, the diaphragm and intercostal muscles contract to enlarge the thorax (chest), decreasing pressure inside the thorax, so that air from the outside of the body enters the lungs. During exhalation, the muscles relax to decrease the volume of the thorax, increasing its internal pressure so that air is pushed out of the lungs.

LATERAL VIEW OF THE LARYNX

The larynx (voice box) links the pharynx with the trachea. It consists of an arrangement of nine pieces of cartilage and has two main functions. First, during swallowing, the upper cartilage (the epiglottis) covers the larynx to stop food from going into the lungs. At other times, the epiglottis is open, and the larynx provides a clear airway. Second, the larynx plays a part in voice production. Sound is produced as vocal folds (cords) vibrate in the air flowing out of the body.

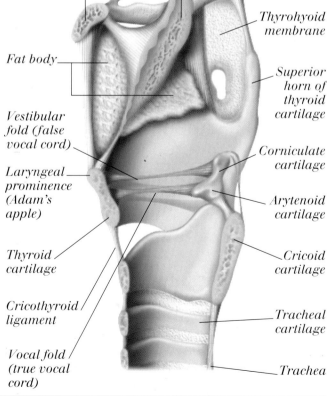

THE RESPIRATORY SYSTEM

The two lungs are located on either side of the heart. The left lung has one oblique fissure, dividing it into superior and inferior lobes. The right lung has two fissures (oblique and horizontal), dividing it into superior, middle, and inferior lobes. Below the lungs, separating the thorax from the abdomen, is a muscular sheet called the diaphragm.

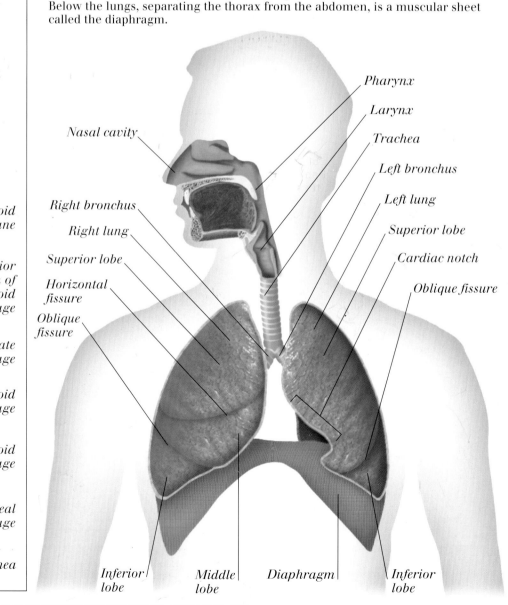

LUNGS

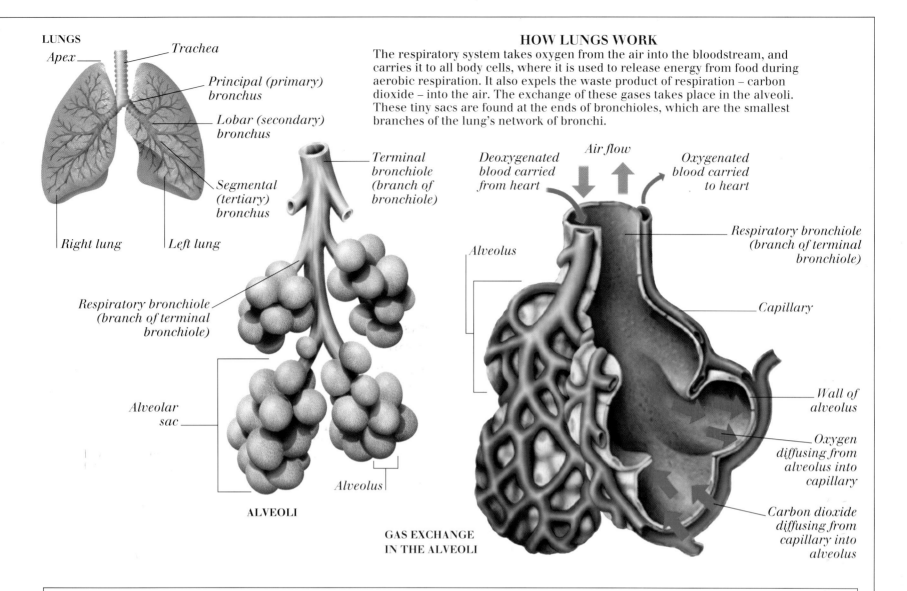

Apex

Trachea

Principal (primary) bronchus

Lobar (secondary) bronchus

Segmental (tertiary) bronchus

Right lung

Left lung

Terminal bronchiole (branch of bronchiole)

Respiratory bronchiole (branch of terminal bronchiole)

Alveolar sac

Alveolus

ALVEOLI

GAS EXCHANGE IN THE ALVEOLI

Alveolus

Deoxygenated blood carried from heart

Air flow

Oxygenated blood carried to heart

Respiratory bronchiole (branch of terminal bronchiole)

Capillary

Wall of alveolus

Oxygen diffusing from alveolus into capillary

Carbon dioxide diffusing from capillary into alveolus

HOW LUNGS WORK

The respiratory system takes oxygen from the air into the bloodstream, and carries it to all body cells, where it is used to release energy from food during aerobic respiration. It also expels the waste product of respiration – carbon dioxide – into the air. The exchange of these gases takes place in the alveoli. These tiny sacs are found at the ends of bronchioles, which are the smallest branches of the lung's network of bronchi.

HOW BREATHING WORKS

BREATHING IN
Breathing moves air in and out of the lungs. During breathing in (inhalation), the diaphragm contracts and flattens, increasing the volume and decreasing the pressure inside the thorax, sucking air into the lungs.

BREATHING OUT
The reverse occurs during breathing out (exhalation). The diaphragm relaxes, reducing the volume and increasing the pressure inside the thorax, forcing air out of the lungs.

RIB ACTION
The ribs also play a part in breathing. During inhalation, the intercostal muscles connecting the ribs contract. This lifts the ribs outward and upward, increasing the volume and decreasing the pressure inside the thorax.

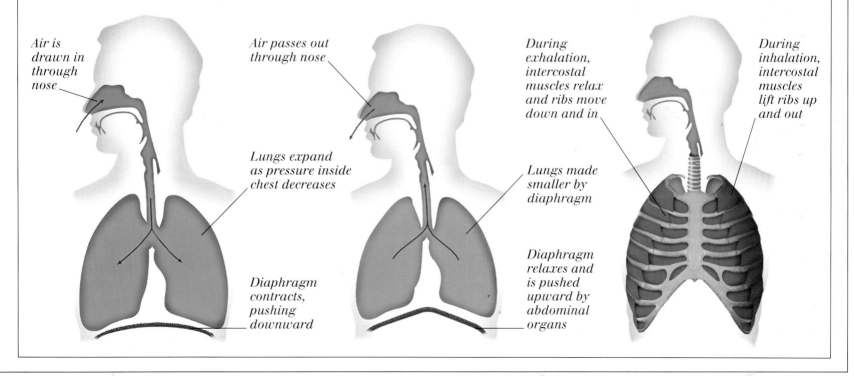

Air is drawn in through nose

Lungs expand as pressure inside chest decreases

Diaphragm contracts, pushing downward

Air passes out through nose

Lungs made smaller by diaphragm

Diaphragm relaxes and is pushed upward by abdominal organs

During exhalation, intercostal muscles relax and ribs move down and in

During inhalation, intercostal muscles lift ribs up and out

Digestive organs

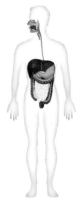

THE DIGESTIVE ORGANS BREAK DOWN food into small nutrient molecules that are used to supply the body's energy needs and the raw materials that are required for growth and repair. Mechanical digestion, such as chewing, breaks down food by physical action; chemical digestion uses digesting agents called enzymes to break down food particles even further. Food ingested through the mouth is cut and ground by the teeth, lubricated with saliva, pushed by the tongue into the pharynx, where it is swallowed, then squeezed down the esophagus into the stomach by muscular action. Here, mechanical and chemical digestion occur, producing a souplike fluid that is released into the small intestine. The digestive process is completed here, assisted by enzyme-containing secretions from the pancreas, as well as bile produced in the liver. Digested food is then absorbed through the small intestine wall into the bloodstream. The large intestine absorbs most of the remaining water from undigested food, which is eliminated through the anus as feces.

SALIVARY GLANDS

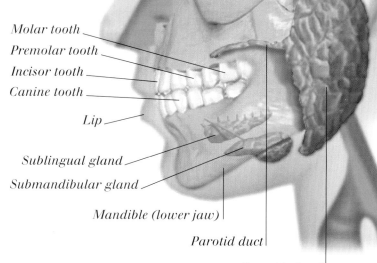

Molar tooth
Premolar tooth
Incisor tooth
Canine tooth
Lip
Sublingual gland
Submandibular gland
Mandible (lower jaw)
Parotid duct
Parotid gland

There are three pairs of salivary glands that release saliva into the mouth through ducts, especially during eating. Saliva moistens and lubricates food, and digests starch.

SWALLOWING

Swallowing, the sequence of movements that takes food from mouth to stomach, has two phases. In the first, the tongue forces the bolus (ball) of chewed-up food backward into the pharynx.

PHASE 1

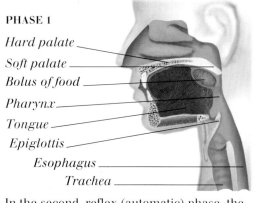

Hard palate
Soft palate
Bolus of food
Pharynx
Tongue
Epiglottis
Esophagus
Trachea

In the second, reflex (automatic) phase, the epiglottis closes to stop food from going into the trachea; the soft palate blocks the entrance to the nasal cavity; and throat muscles push the food bolus into the esophagus.

PHASE 2

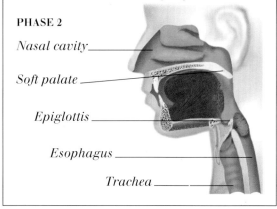

Nasal cavity
Soft palate
Epiglottis
Esophagus
Trachea

THE DIGESTIVE SYSTEM

The digestive system has two parts: the alimentary canal, formed by the mouth, pharynx (throat), esophagus, stomach, and small and large intestine; and the accessory organs, formed by the salivary glands, teeth, tongue, liver, gallbladder, and pancreas.

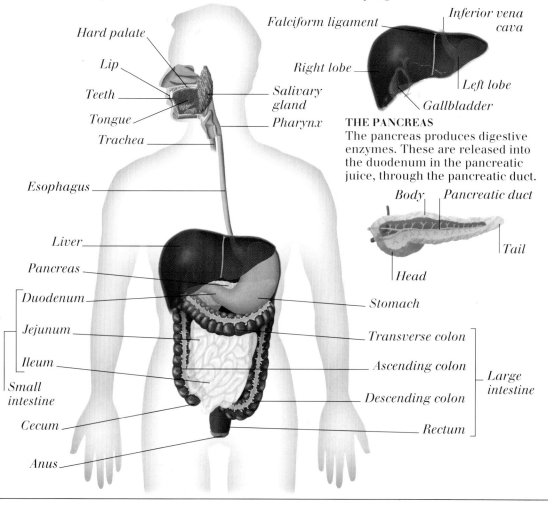

Hard palate
Lip
Teeth
Tongue
Trachea
Esophagus
Liver
Pancreas
Duodenum
Jejunum
Ileum
Small intestine
Cecum
Anus
Salivary gland
Pharynx
Stomach
Transverse colon
Ascending colon
Descending colon
Rectum
Large intestine

LIVER AND GALLBLADDER

The liver produces bile, which is stored in the gallbladder and emptied into the duodenum to help digest fats.

Falciform ligament
Inferior vena cava
Right lobe
Left lobe
Gallbladder

THE PANCREAS

The pancreas produces digestive enzymes. These are released into the duodenum in the pancreatic juice, through the pancreatic duct.

Body
Pancreatic duct
Tail
Head

TEETH

Teeth cut and crush food so that it can be swallowed and digested more easily. A tooth has an outer layer of hard enamel overlying a layer of bonelike dentine, which encloses the pulp cavity.

MOLAR TOOTH

Enamel

Dentine

Pulp cavity

Gum

Cementum

Periodontal ligament

Blood vessel

Crown

Neck

Root

Nerve

Esophagus

Circular muscles contract

Circular muscles relax

Bolus of food

ESOPHAGUS WITH FOOD BOLUS

PERISTALSIS

This is the process that moves food along the alimentary canal toward the stomach. After swallowing, for example, the circular muscle that surrounds the esophagus contracts behind the food but relaxes in front of it. As this powerful wave of contraction moves toward the stomach, it pushes the food forward.

THE STOMACH

The stomach stores food for several hours, during which time its muscular wall contracts to churn up food, and its digestive juices work to break down proteins. This partially digests food into a souplike liquid, which is then released into the duodenum.

INTERIOR VIEW OF STOMACH

Esophagus

Cardiac sphincter

Cardiac region of stomach

Pylorus

Pyloric sphincter

Duodenum (first part of small intestine)

Fundus of stomach

Stomach wall

Body of stomach

Rugae (folds)

THE SMALL INTESTINE

This is the part of the alimentary canal where digestion is completed with the aid of enzymes secreted by the intestinal wall. Microscopic projections called villi give the small intestine wall a larger surface area to make the absorption of food more efficient.

From stomach

Bile duct

Accessory pancreatic duct

Main pancreatic duct

Digesting food

Duodenum

Jejunum

Wall of small intestine

To large intestine

Lining of the small intestine

Ileum

Capillary network

Villus

Lacteal

SURFACE OF SMALL INTESTINE

THE LARGE INTESTINE

This carries undigested waste out of the body. Water is absorbed from liquid waste as it passes through the colon, leaving only solid feces. These are stored in the rectum before being released through the anus.

Haustrum

Transverse colon

Colon wall

Ascending colon

Ileocecal valve

From small intestine

Descending colon

Cecum

Ileum

Appendix

Rectum

Anus

Taenia coli

Sigmoid colon

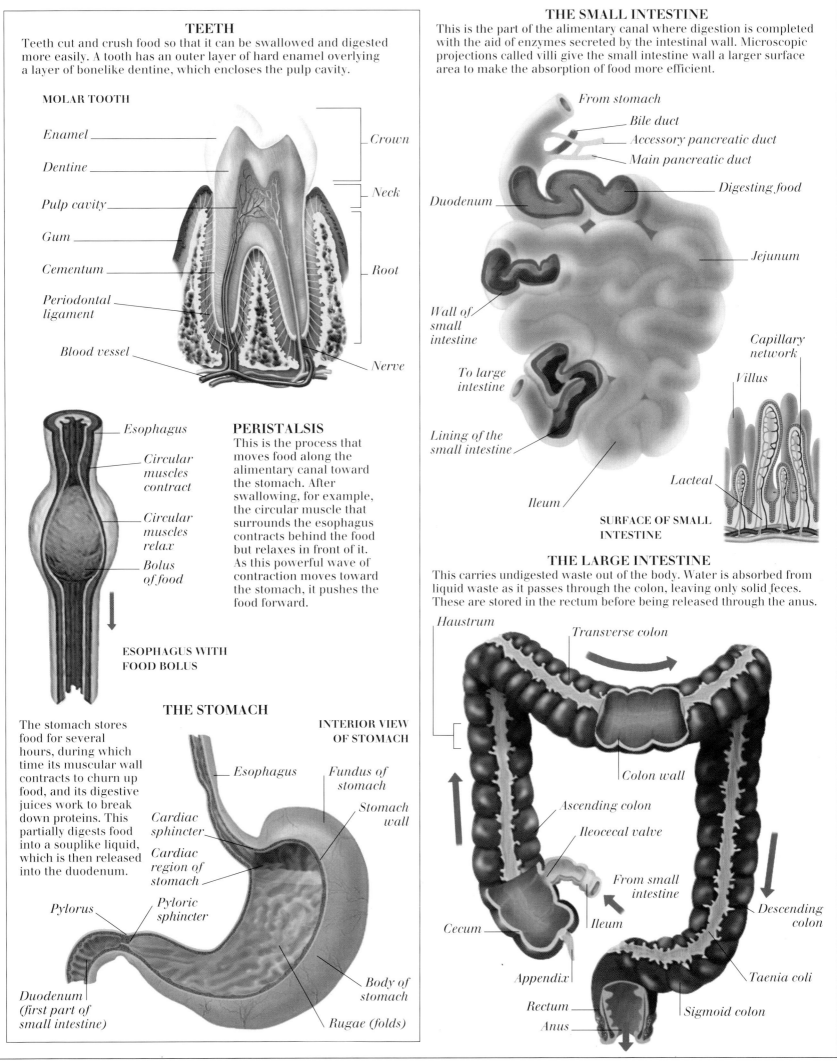

Urinary and reproductive systems

THE URINARY SYSTEM, which consists of the urinary bladder, ureters, urethra, and kidneys, produces urine, a waste liquid, and transports it out of the body. Urine forms as the two kidneys remove all water and salts in excess of the body's requirements, along with urea (a waste substance produced by the liver), and other poisonous wastes from the blood. Urine flows down the ureters to the muscular bladder which, when full, gently squeezes it out of the body through the urethra. The reproductive system works by generating and transporting male and female sex cells (sperm or ova) with the purpose of producing offspring. The male reproductive system consists of two sperm-producing testes, the vasa deferentia (sing. vas deferens), the urethra and erectile penis, and semen-producing glands, including the prostate. The female reproductive system consists of two ovaries, which alternately release one ovum (egg) each month, the uterine tubes, the uterus, and the vagina. The male and female reproductive systems are brought together when the erect penis is placed inside the vagina during sexual intercourse. Sperm, activated by semen, are transported along the vasa deferentia and ejaculated from the penis. They then swim through the uterus, and fertilize an ovum, if present, in the uterine tubes.

THE URINARY SYSTEM

Over a million filtration units called nephrons, found in the kidney's medulla and cortex, daily process up to 47.5 gallons (180 liters) of fluid from blood to produce about 3.2 pints (1.5 liters) of urine. This passes down the ureter and is stored in the bladder.

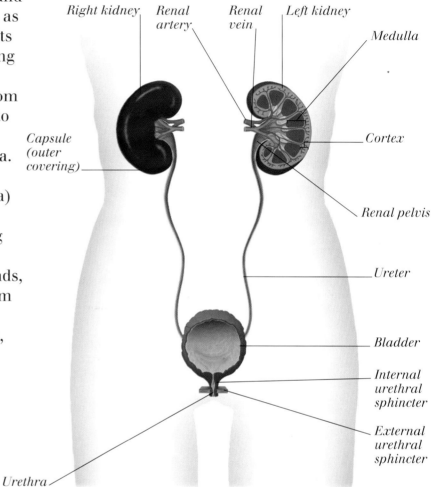

Right kidney
Renal artery
Renal vein
Left kidney
Medulla
Capsule (outer covering)
Cortex
Renal pelvis
Ureter
Bladder
Internal urethral sphincter
External urethral sphincter
Urethra

HOW KIDNEYS WORK

Tiny blood-processing units (nephrons) collect fluid from the blood through glomerular capsules. Useful substances are reabsorbed into the blood as the fluid passes through the tubules. When it reaches the collecting duct, it contains only waste (urine).

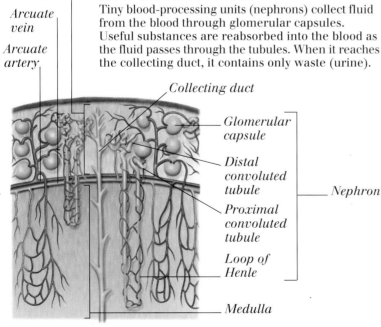

Cortex
Arcuate vein
Arcuate artery
Collecting duct
Glomerular capsule
Distal convoluted tubule
Nephron
Proximal convoluted tubule
Loop of Henle
Medulla

THE BLADDER

As the bladder fills with urine, it expands and triggers a conscious urge to urinate. The two sphincters (muscle rings) are relaxed, the bladder contracts rhythmically, and urine is expelled along the urethra.

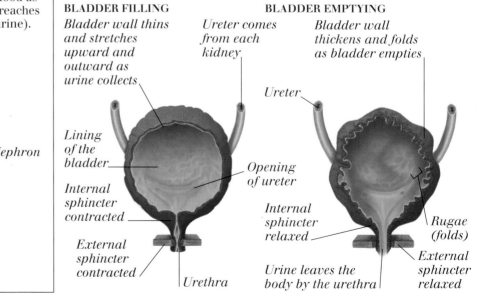

BLADDER FILLING
Bladder wall thins and stretches upward and outward as urine collects
Lining of the bladder
Internal sphincter contracted
External sphincter contracted

BLADDER EMPTYING
Ureter comes from each kidney
Bladder wall thickens and folds as bladder empties
Ureter
Opening of ureter
Internal sphincter relaxed
Rugae (folds)
External sphincter relaxed
Urine leaves the body by the urethra
Urethra

REPRODUCTIVE ORGANS

FEMALE REPRODUCTIVE ORGANS

Each month, one ovary releases an ovum, and the endometrium (lining of the uterus) thickens in preparation to receive the ovum, should it be fertilized in the uterine tube on its way to the uterus. The vagina is the canal through which sperm enter a woman's body and through which a baby is born.

MALE REPRODUCTIVE ORGANS

The testes produce millions of sperm each day. On their way to the penis along the vasa deferentia (sing. vas deferens), sperm are mixed with fluid from the seminal vesicles and prostate gland to form semen. The penis contains spongy tissue that fills with blood before sexual intercourse, making the penis erect.

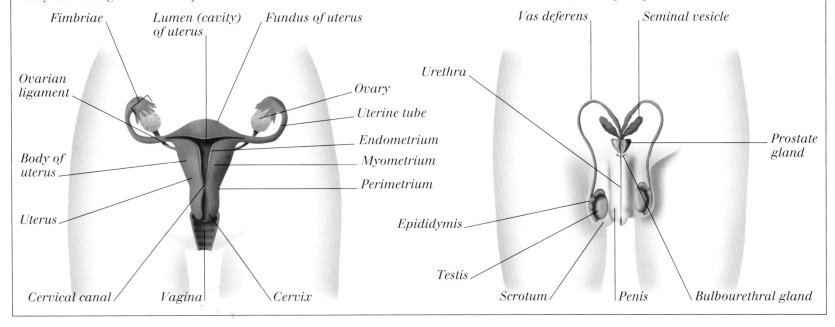

HOW REPRODUCTION WORKS

SEXUAL INTERCOURSE

Sexual intercourse (coitus) is the act that brings male and female sex cells into contact. When a couple becomes sexually aroused, a man puts his erect penis inside his partner's vagina. As they move together, the man ejaculates, releasing semen into the vagina. Sperm in the semen swim through the cervix, into the uterus, and up to the uterine tubes.

FERTILIZATION OF THE OVUM

The union of the ovum with a single sperm produces a zygote (fertilized ovum) that will develop into a baby in the uterus. For fertilization to occur, sperm must reach the ovum within 24 hours of its release from the ovary.

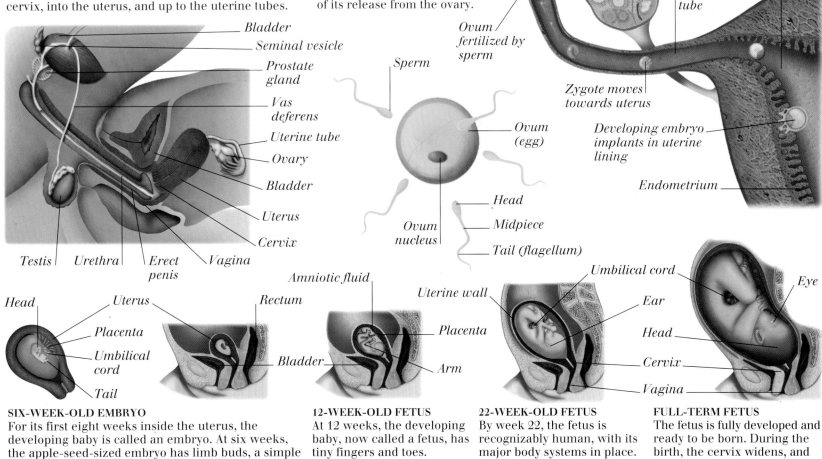

SIX-WEEK-OLD EMBRYO

For its first eight weeks inside the uterus, the developing baby is called an embryo. At six weeks, the apple-seed-sized embryo has limb buds, a simple brain, and eyes. It obtains food and oxygen from its mother through the placenta and umbilical cord.

12-WEEK-OLD FETUS

At 12 weeks, the developing baby, now called a fetus, has tiny fingers and toes. Amniotic fluid protects it from external shocks.

22-WEEK-OLD FETUS

By week 22, the fetus is recognizably human, with its major body systems in place. Its kicking movements can be felt by the mother.

FULL-TERM FETUS

The fetus is fully developed and ready to be born. During the birth, the cervix widens, and the uterus muscles contract to push the baby out of the vagina.

Head and neck 1

THE HEAD CONTAINS THE BRAIN – the body's control center – and major sense organs. Its framework is provided by the skull, which is made up of the cranium and the facial bones. The cranium encloses and protects both the brain and the organs of hearing and balance. The facial bones form the face and provide the openings through which air and food enter the body. They also contain the organs of smell and taste, hold the teeth in place, house and protect the eyes, and provide attachment points for the facial muscles. The neck supports the head and provides a conduit for communication between the head and trunk. Blood is carried to and from the head by the carotid arteries and jugular veins. The spinal cord, which links the brain to the rest of the nervous system, runs protected within a tunnel formed by the cervical vertebrae. The trachea (windpipe) carries air between the pharynx (throat) and lungs. The esophagus transports food from the pharynx to the stomach.

SUPERFICIAL AND DEEP FACIAL MUSCLES

These muscles produce the wide range of facial expressions that communicate thoughts and emotions. These muscles include the frontalis, which wrinkles the forehead; the orbicularis oculi, which causes blinking; the risorius, which pulls the edge of the lip sideways into a smile; and the depressor labii inferioris, which pulls the lower lip downward into a pout.

Galea aponeurotica

Frontalis

Corrugator supercilii

Tendon of superior oblique

Lacrimal sac

Levator palpebrae superioris

Temporalis

Superior tarsal plate

Lacrimal gland

Inferior tarsal plate

Orbital fat

Orbicularis oculi

Zygomaticus minor

Zygomaticus major

Levator labii superioris

Parotid gland

Buccinator

Levator anguli oris

Masseter

Depressor labii inferioris

Depressor anguli oris

Procerus

Orbicularis oculi

Nasalis

Levator labii superioris alaeque nasi

Zygomaticus minor

Levator labii superioris

Depressor septi

Zygomaticus major

Orbicularis oris

Risorius

Platysma

Depressor anguli oris

Depressor labii inferioris

Mentalis

SUPERFICIAL MUSCLES

DEEP MUSCLES

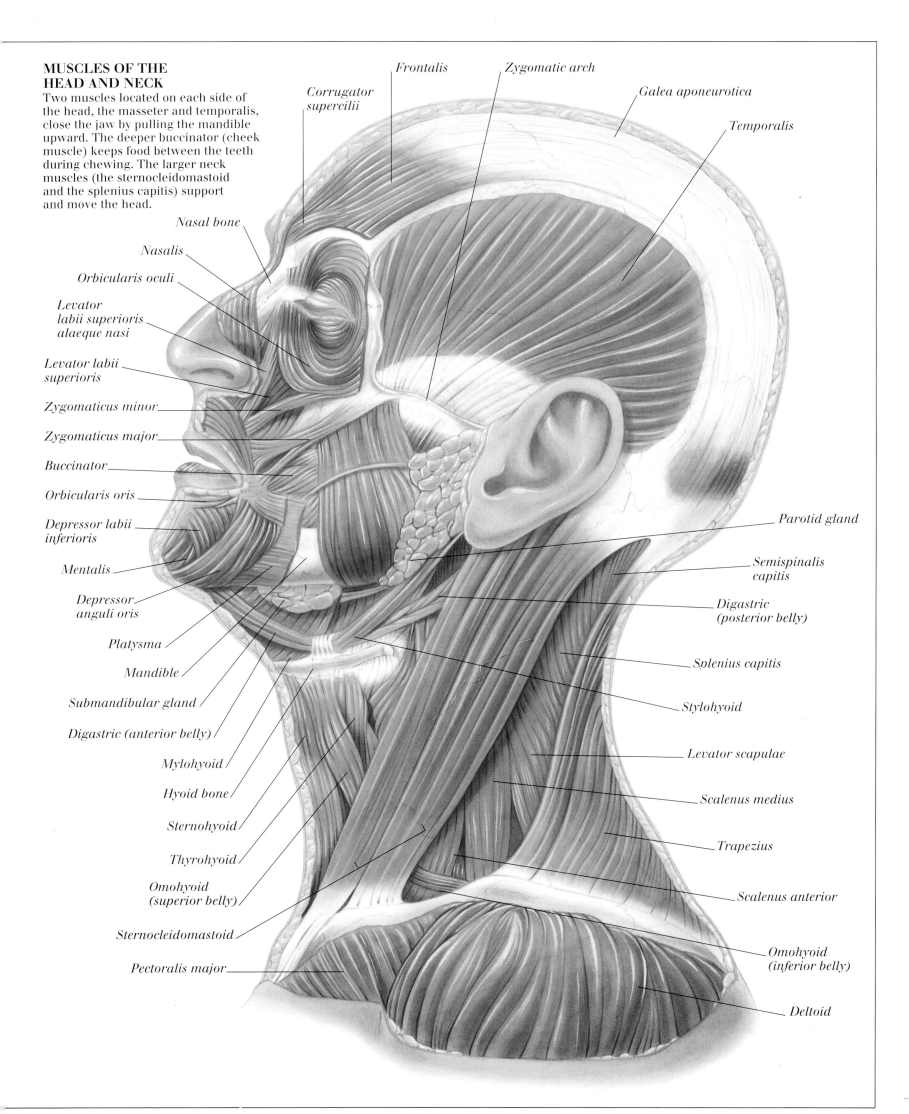

MUSCLES OF THE HEAD AND NECK

Two muscles located on each side of the head, the masseter and temporalis, close the jaw by pulling the mandible upward. The deeper buccinator (cheek muscle) keeps food between the teeth during chewing. The larger neck muscles (the sternocleidomastoid and the splenius capitis) support and move the head.

Corrugator supercilii

Frontalis

Zygomatic arch

Galea aponeurotica

Temporalis

Nasal bone

Nasalis

Orbicularis oculi

Levator labii superioris alaeque nasi

Levator labii superioris

Zygomaticus minor

Zygomaticus major

Buccinator

Orbicularis oris

Depressor labii inferioris

Mentalis

Depressor anguli oris

Platysma

Mandible

Submandibular gland

Digastric (anterior belly)

Mylohyoid

Hyoid bone

Sternohyoid

Thyrohyoid

Omohyoid (superior belly)

Sternocleidomastoid

Pectoralis major

Parotid gland

Semispinalis capitis

Digastric (posterior belly)

Splenius capitis

Stylohyoid

Levator scapulae

Scalenus medius

Trapezius

Scalenus anterior

Omohyoid (inferior belly)

Deltoid

Head and neck 2

SUPERFICIAL MUSCLES, NERVES, AND BLOOD VESSELS
Branches of the facial nerve control the muscles of facial
expression, such as the risorius. Blood is supplied
to and from most parts of the head by branches
of the external carotid arteries and internal
jugular veins. These include the facial and
superficial temporal arteries and veins.

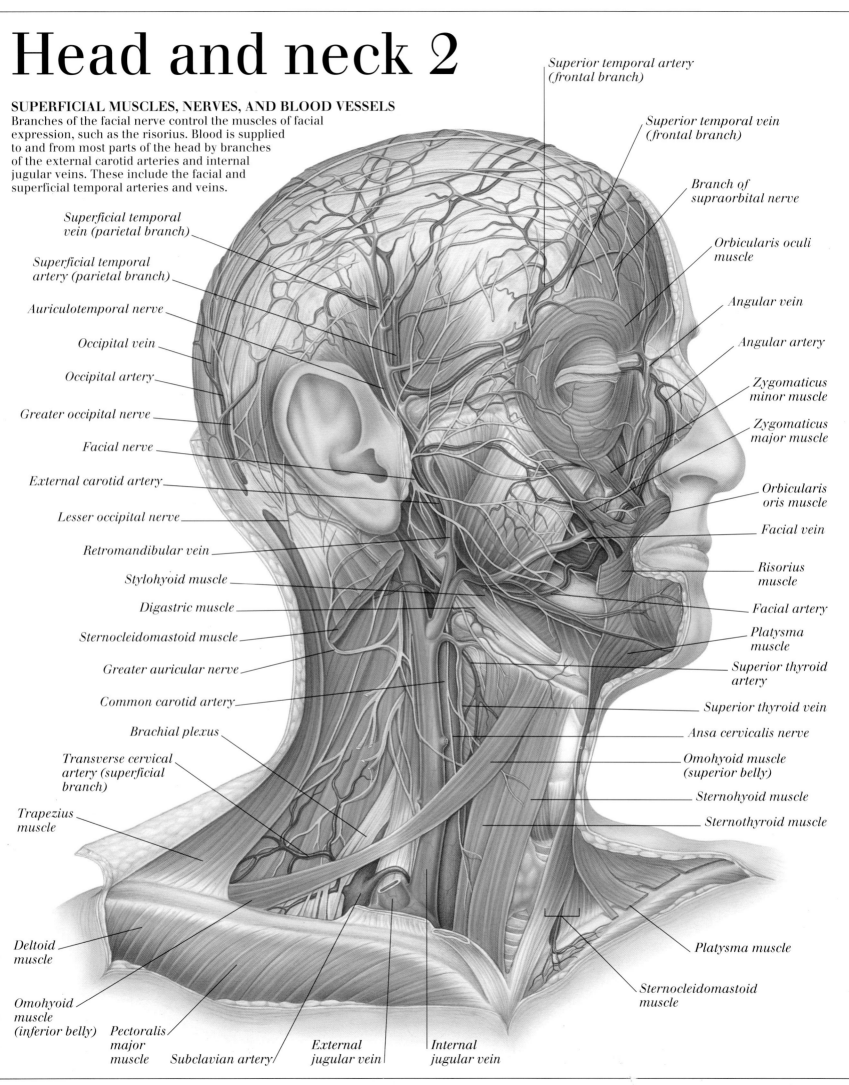

Superficial temporal
vein (parietal branch)

Superficial temporal
artery (parietal branch)

Auriculotemporal nerve

Occipital vein

Occipital artery

Greater occipital nerve

Facial nerve

External carotid artery

Lesser occipital nerve

Retromandibular vein

Stylohyoid muscle

Digastric muscle

Sternocleidomastoid muscle

Greater auricular nerve

Common carotid artery

Brachial plexus

Transverse cervical
artery (superficial
branch)

Trapezius
muscle

Deltoid
muscle

Omohyoid
muscle
(inferior belly)

Pectoralis
major
muscle

Subclavian artery

External
jugular vein

Internal
jugular vein

Superior temporal vein
(frontal branch)

Branch of
supraorbital nerve

Orbicularis oculi
muscle

Angular vein

Angular artery

Zygomaticus
minor muscle

Zygomaticus
major muscle

Orbicularis
oris muscle

Facial vein

Risorius
muscle

Facial artery

Platysma
muscle

Superior thyroid
artery

Superior thyroid vein

Ansa cervicalis nerve

Omohyoid muscle
(superior belly)

Sternohyoid muscle

Sternothyroid muscle

Platysma muscle

Sternocleidomastoid
muscle

POSTERIOR VIEW OF THE NECK AND HEAD

The head is balanced on top of the vertebral column. The muscles of the posterior of the neck, such as the splenius capitis and semispinalis capitis, assisted by the trapezius, support the head by pulling it back to prevent it from falling forward.

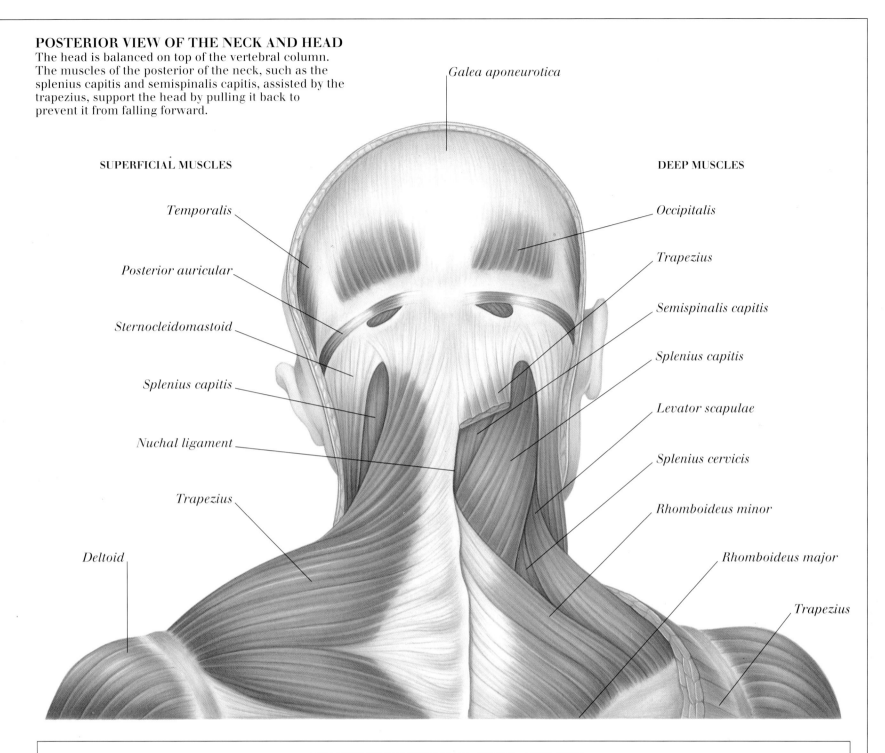

Galea aponeurotica

SUPERFICIAL MUSCLES

Temporalis

Posterior auricular

Sternocleidomastoid

Splenius capitis

Nuchal ligament

Trapezius

Deltoid

DEEP MUSCLES

Occipitalis

Trapezius

Semispinalis capitis

Splenius capitis

Levator scapulae

Splenius cervicis

Rhomboideus minor

Rhomboideus major

Trapezius

ANATOMY OF THE EAR, NOSE, AND EYE

EAR
The middle section of the ear is traversed by three small bones, which carry sounds to the cochlea, where they are converted into nerve impulses and then carried to the brain for interpretation.

NOSE
The framework of the external nose has a bony part, consisting mainly of the nasal bones, and a more flexible cartilaginous part, consisting of the lateral, septal, and alar cartilages.

EYE
The spherical eyeball consists of a tough outer layer (the sclera) with a clear cornea at the front. It is moved up and down, and from side to side by four rectus and two oblique muscles.

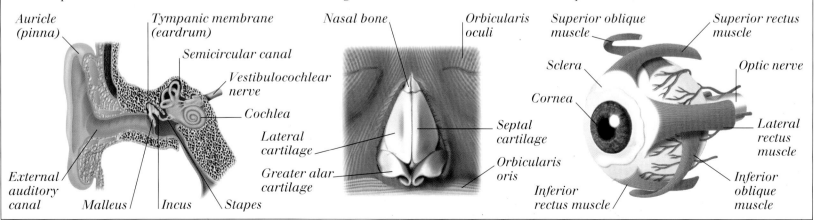

Auricle (pinna)

Tympanic membrane (eardrum)

Semicircular canal

Vestibulocochlear nerve

Cochlea

External auditory canal

Malleus

Incus

Stapes

Nasal bone

Orbicularis oculi

Lateral cartilage

Greater alar cartilage

Septal cartilage

Orbicularis oris

Superior oblique muscle

Superior rectus muscle

Sclera

Optic nerve

Cornea

Lateral rectus muscle

Inferior rectus muscle

Inferior oblique muscle

Head and neck 3

The removal of the skull bones reveals three sense organs: the eye, nasal cavity, and tongue. The muscles of the neck rotate the head and bend it to the side. The epiglottis closes the entrance to the trachea during swallowing to stop food from entering it.

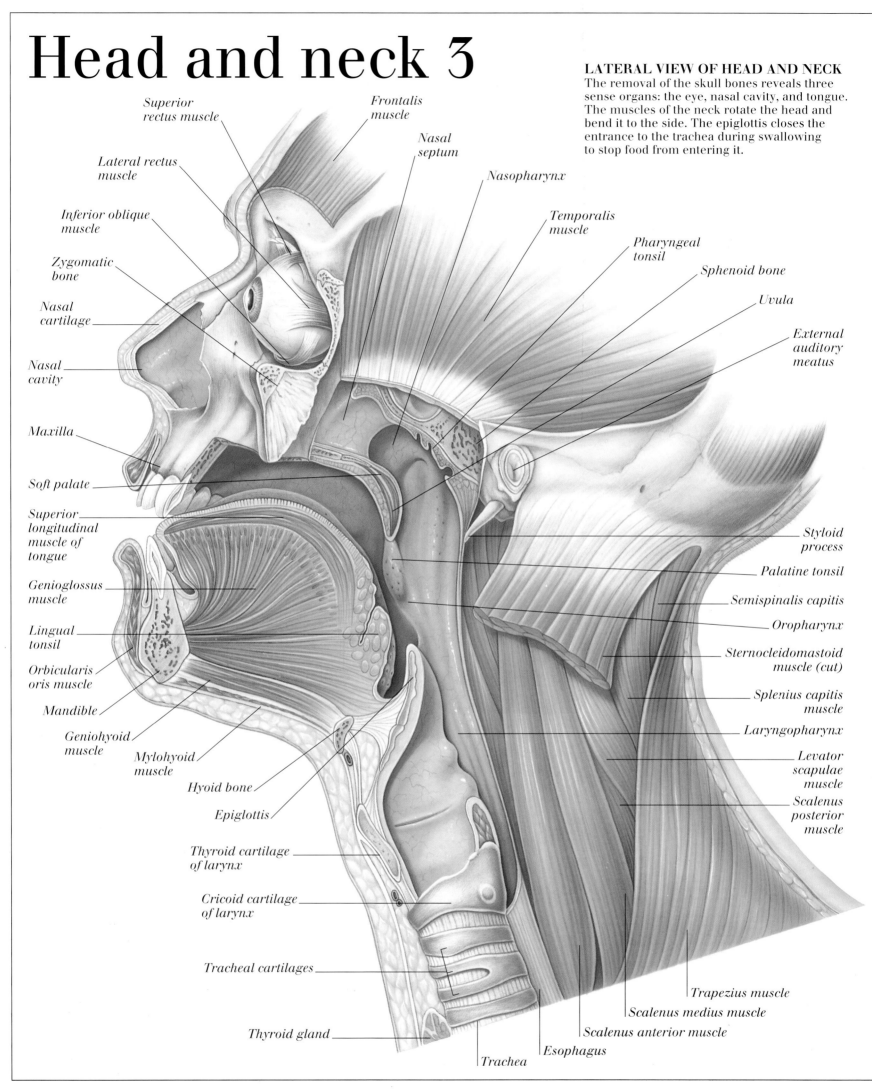

Superior rectus muscle

Lateral rectus muscle

Inferior oblique muscle

Zygomatic bone

Nasal cartilage

Nasal cavity

Maxilla

Soft palate

Superior longitudinal muscle of tongue

Genioglossus muscle

Lingual tonsil

Orbicularis oris muscle

Mandible

Geniohyoid muscle

Mylohyoid muscle

Hyoid bone

Epiglottis

Thyroid cartilage of larynx

Cricoid cartilage of larynx

Tracheal cartilages

Thyroid gland

Trachea

Frontalis muscle

Nasal septum

Nasopharynx

Temporalis muscle

Pharyngeal tonsil

Sphenoid bone

Uvula

External auditory meatus

Styloid process

Palatine tonsil

Semispinalis capitis

Oropharynx

Sternocleidomastoid muscle (cut)

Splenius capitis muscle

Laryngopharynx

Levator scapulae muscle

Scalenus posterior muscle

Trapezius muscle

Scalenus medius muscle

Scalenus anterior muscle

Esophagus

HOW THE NOSE, TONGUE, AND EYE WORK

NOSE
The nose is used for breathing and smelling. Smell receptors in the olfactory epithelium, which lines the upper nasal cavity, detect odor molecules in the air passing over them.

TONGUE
The tongue is a muscular organ used to swallow and taste food. Tastes are detected by taste buds located on papillae, protuberances on the tongue.

EYE
The eye enables us to see our surroundings. Light enters, and is focused by, the cornea and lens, and is detected by sensors in the retina, which send nerve impulses to the brain.

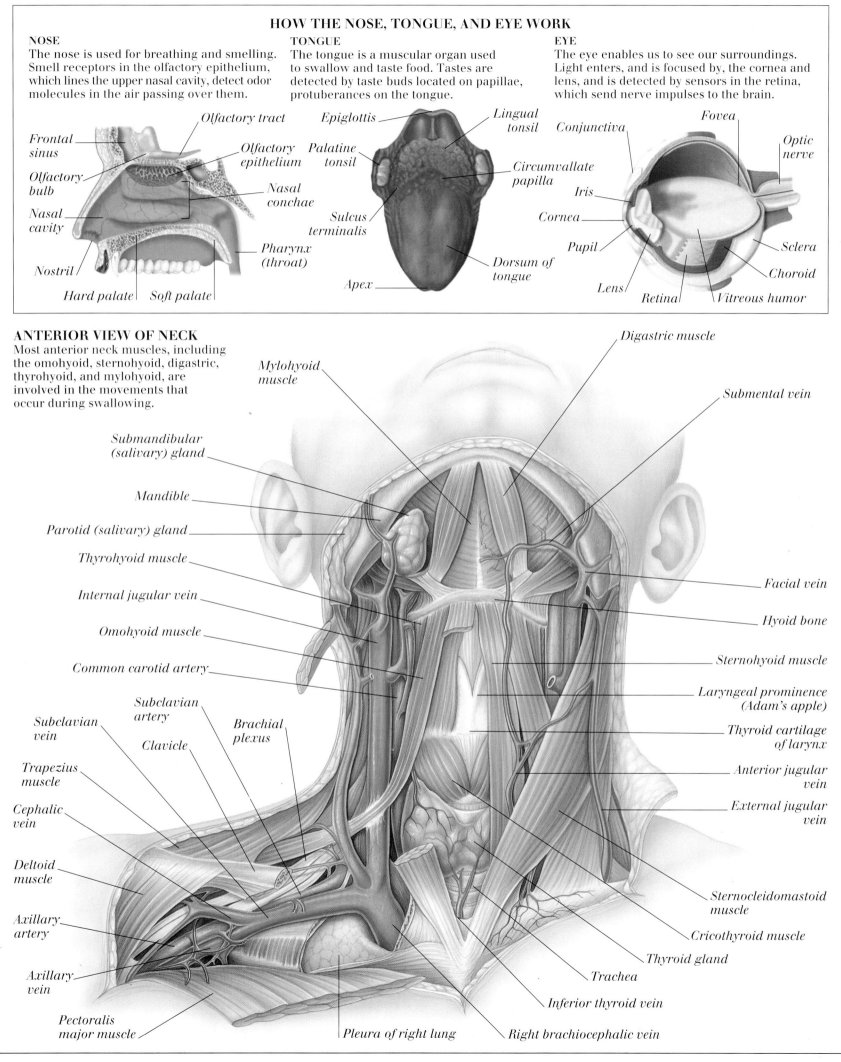

Olfactory tract

Frontal sinus

Olfactory epithelium

Olfactory bulb

Nasal conchae

Nasal cavity

Nostril

Hard palate

Soft palate

Epiglottis

Palatine tonsil

Lingual tonsil

Circumvallate papilla

Sulcus terminalis

Pharynx (throat)

Apex

Dorsum of tongue

Conjunctiva

Fovea

Optic nerve

Iris

Cornea

Pupil

Lens

Retina

Sclera

Choroid

Vitreous humor

ANTERIOR VIEW OF NECK
Most anterior neck muscles, including the omohyoid, sternohyoid, digastric, thyrohyoid, and mylohyoid, are involved in the movements that occur during swallowing.

Mylohyoid muscle

Digastric muscle

Submental vein

Submandibular (salivary) gland

Mandible

Parotid (salivary) gland

Thyrohyoid muscle

Internal jugular vein

Omohyoid muscle

Common carotid artery

Subclavian artery

Subclavian vein

Clavicle

Brachial plexus

Trapezius muscle

Cephalic vein

Deltoid muscle

Axillary artery

Axillary vein

Pectoralis major muscle

Pleura of right lung

Right brachiocephalic vein

Inferior thyroid vein

Trachea

Thyroid gland

Cricothyroid muscle

Sternocleidomastoid muscle

External jugular vein

Anterior jugular vein

Thyroid cartilage of larynx

Laryngeal prominence (Adam's apple)

Sternohyoid muscle

Hyoid bone

Facial vein

Head and neck 4

ANTERIOR VIEW OF SKULL
The skull is made up of 22 bones. Cranial bones, such as the frontal bone, form the helmetlike cranium; facial bones, such as the maxilla, form the face.

POSTERIOR VIEW OF SKULL
Skull bones, apart from the mandible (lower jaw), are fused together at interlocking joints called sutures, which stop the bones from moving.

INFERIOR VIEW OF SKULL
The foramen magnum is a large hole through which the brain connects to the spinal cord. The occipital condyles form a joint with the top of the backbone.

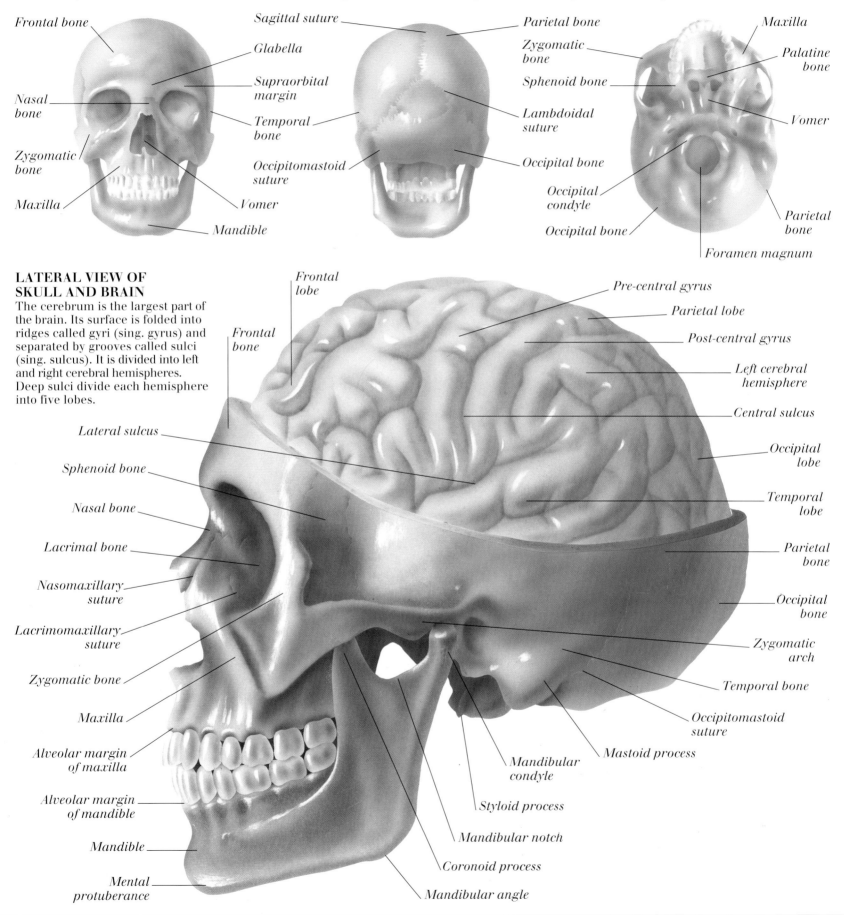

Frontal bone
Glabella
Supraorbital margin
Nasal bone
Temporal bone
Zygomatic bone
Maxilla
Vomer
Mandible

Sagittal suture
Occipitomastoid suture

Parietal bone
Zygomatic bone
Sphenoid bone
Lambdoidal suture
Occipital bone

Maxilla
Palatine bone
Vomer
Occipital condyle
Occipital bone
Parietal bone
Foramen magnum

LATERAL VIEW OF SKULL AND BRAIN
The cerebrum is the largest part of the brain. Its surface is folded into ridges called gyri (sing. gyrus) and separated by grooves called sulci (sing. sulcus). It is divided into left and right cerebral hemispheres. Deep sulci divide each hemisphere into five lobes.

Frontal lobe
Frontal bone
Lateral sulcus
Sphenoid bone
Nasal bone
Lacrimal bone
Nasomaxillary suture
Lacrimomaxillary suture
Zygomatic bone
Maxilla
Alveolar margin of maxilla
Alveolar margin of mandible
Mandible
Mental protuberance

Pre-central gyrus
Parietal lobe
Post-central gyrus
Left cerebral hemisphere
Central sulcus
Occipital lobe
Temporal lobe
Parietal bone
Occipital bone
Zygomatic arch
Temporal bone
Occipitomastoid suture
Mastoid process
Mandibular condyle
Styloid process
Mandibular notch
Coronoid process
Mandibular angle

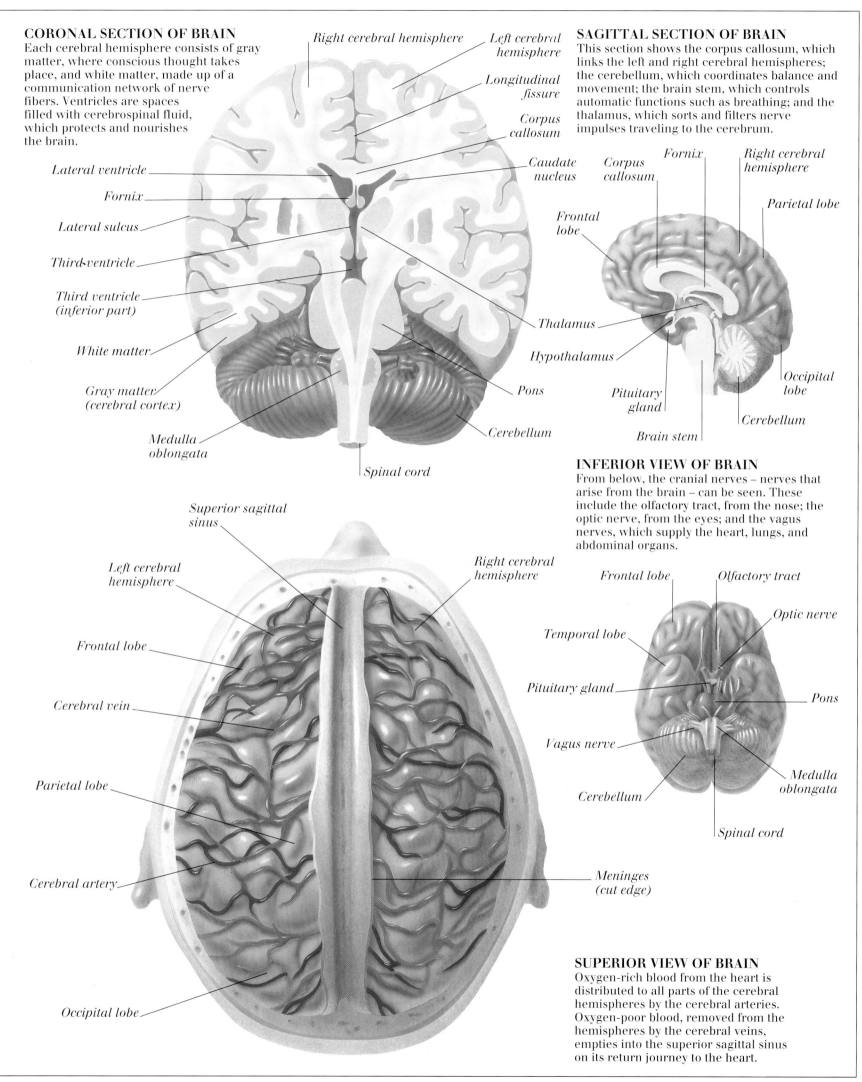

CORONAL SECTION OF BRAIN
Each cerebral hemisphere consists of gray matter, where conscious thought takes place, and white matter, made up of a communication network of nerve fibers. Ventricles are spaces filled with cerebrospinal fluid, which protects and nourishes the brain.

Right cerebral hemisphere

Left cerebral hemisphere

Longitudinal fissure

Corpus callosum

Caudate nucleus

Lateral ventricle

Fornix

Lateral sulcus

Third ventricle

Third ventricle (inferior part)

White matter

Gray matter (cerebral cortex)

Medulla oblongata

Spinal cord

Thalamus

Pons

Cerebellum

SAGITTAL SECTION OF BRAIN
This section shows the corpus callosum, which links the left and right cerebral hemispheres; the cerebellum, which coordinates balance and movement; the brain stem, which controls automatic functions such as breathing; and the thalamus, which sorts and filters nerve impulses traveling to the cerebrum.

Corpus callosum

Fornix

Right cerebral hemisphere

Parietal lobe

Frontal lobe

Hypothalamus

Pituitary gland

Brain stem

Occipital lobe

Cerebellum

INFERIOR VIEW OF BRAIN
From below, the cranial nerves – nerves that arise from the brain – can be seen. These include the olfactory tract, from the nose; the optic nerve, from the eyes; and the vagus nerves, which supply the heart, lungs, and abdominal organs.

Frontal lobe

Olfactory tract

Optic nerve

Temporal lobe

Pituitary gland

Pons

Vagus nerve

Cerebellum

Medulla oblongata

Spinal cord

Superior sagittal sinus

Right cerebral hemisphere

Left cerebral hemisphere

Frontal lobe

Cerebral vein

Parietal lobe

Cerebral artery

Occipital lobe

Meninges (cut edge)

SUPERIOR VIEW OF BRAIN
Oxygen-rich blood from the heart is distributed to all parts of the cerebral hemispheres by the cerebral arteries. Oxygen-poor blood, removed from the hemispheres by the cerebral veins, empties into the superior sagittal sinus on its return journey to the heart.

Trunk 1

THE TRUNK, OR TORSO, IS THE CENTRAL part of the body, to which the head, arms, and legs are attached. It is divided into an upper thorax, or chest, and a lower abdomen. Major superficial muscles of the anterior trunk include the pectoralis major, which pulls the arm forward and inward, and the external oblique, which holds in the contents of the abdomen and flexes the trunk. Major deep muscles include the external intercostals, which move the ribs upward during breathing, and the rectus abdominis, which flexes the lower back. Women have breasts – soft, fleshy domes that surround the mammary glands overlying the pectoralis major muscle. Each breast consists of lobes of milk-secreting glands, which are supported by ligaments and embedded in fat, with ducts that open out of the body through the nipple. Major superficial muscles of the posterior trunk include the trapezius, which stabilizes the shoulder, and the latissimus dorsi, which pulls the arm backward and inward. Major deep muscles include the rhomboid minor and rhomboid major, which "square the shoulders." The trunk has a bony axis, which is known as the vertebral column, or spine. Spinal nerves emerge from the spinal cord, which is protected within the spine.

SAGITTAL SECTION OF LEFT BREAST
After a baby is born, the mother begins to produce milk (lactate). The milk is made by the glands in the lobules, and accumulates in the lactiferous sinuses. It is released from the sinuses through the lactiferous ducts when the baby sucks on the nipple.

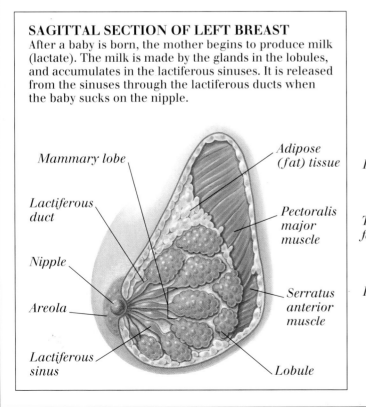

Mammary lobe

Lactiferous duct

Nipple

Areola

Lactiferous sinus

Adipose (fat) tissue

Pectoralis major muscle

Serratus anterior muscle

Lobule

LATERAL VIEW OF SUPERFICIAL MUSCLES
The lateral view of the trunk shows two powerful muscles that act as antagonists (work in opposite directions to one another): the latissimus dorsi, which extends the arm, pulling it backward, and the pectoralis major, which, assisted by the biceps brachii, flexes the arm and pulls it forward.

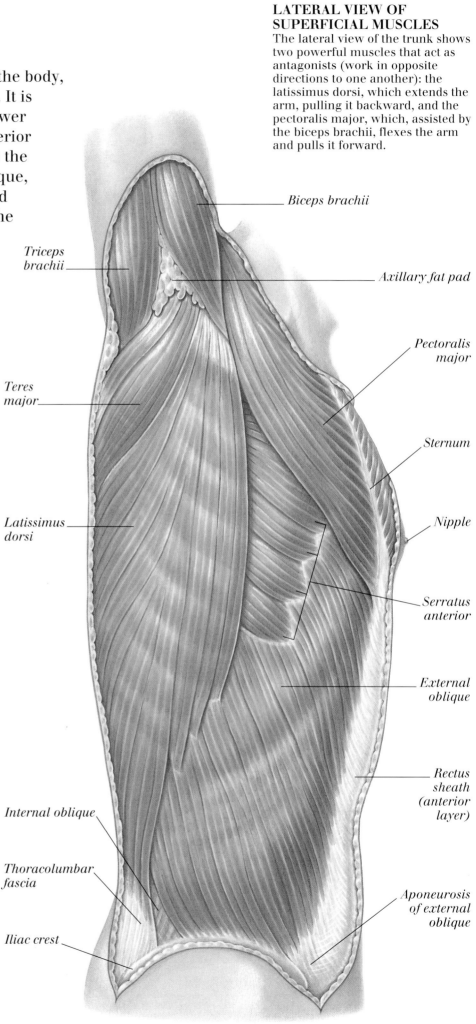

Triceps brachii

Teres major

Latissimus dorsi

Internal oblique

Thoracolumbar fascia

Iliac crest

Biceps brachii

Axillary fat pad

Pectoralis major

Sternum

Nipple

Serratus anterior

External oblique

Rectus sheath (anterior layer)

Aponeurosis of external oblique

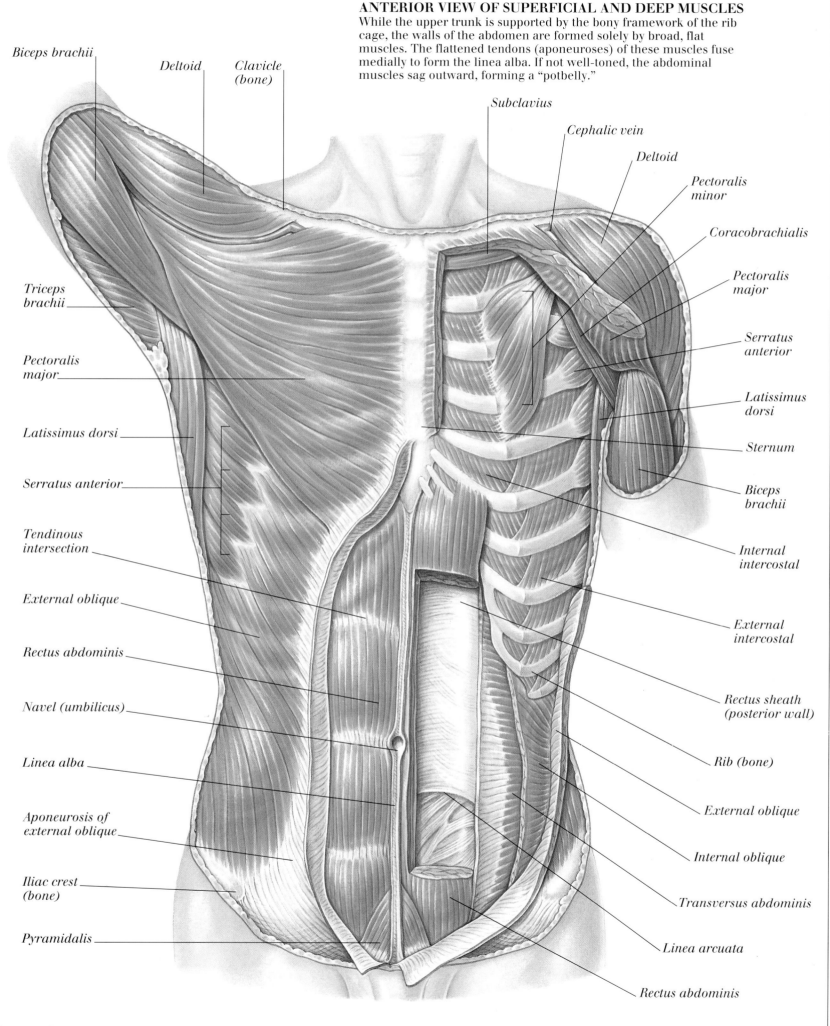

ANTERIOR VIEW OF SUPERFICIAL AND DEEP MUSCLES
While the upper trunk is supported by the bony framework of the rib cage, the walls of the abdomen are formed solely by broad, flat muscles. The flattened tendons (aponeuroses) of these muscles fuse medially to form the linea alba. If not well-toned, the abdominal muscles sag outward, forming a "potbelly."

Biceps brachii

Deltoid

Clavicle (bone)

Subclavius

Cephalic vein

Deltoid

Pectoralis minor

Coracobrachialis

Pectoralis major

Triceps brachii

Serratus anterior

Pectoralis major

Latissimus dorsi

Latissimus dorsi

Sternum

Serratus anterior

Biceps brachii

Tendinous intersection

Internal intercostal

External oblique

External intercostal

Rectus abdominis

Navel (umbilicus)

Rectus sheath (posterior wall)

Linea alba

Rib (bone)

Aponeurosis of external oblique

External oblique

Internal oblique

Iliac crest (bone)

Transversus abdominis

Pyramidalis

Linea arcuata

Rectus abdominis

SUPERFICIAL MUSCLES

DEEP MUSCLES

Trunk 2

POSTERIOR VIEW OF SUPERFICIAL AND DEEP MUSCLES

The superficial back muscles move the arms and shoulders. The deep erector spinae muscles act to extend (straighten) the back by pulling the trunk upward to an erect position, and to control back flexion (bending forward at the waist).

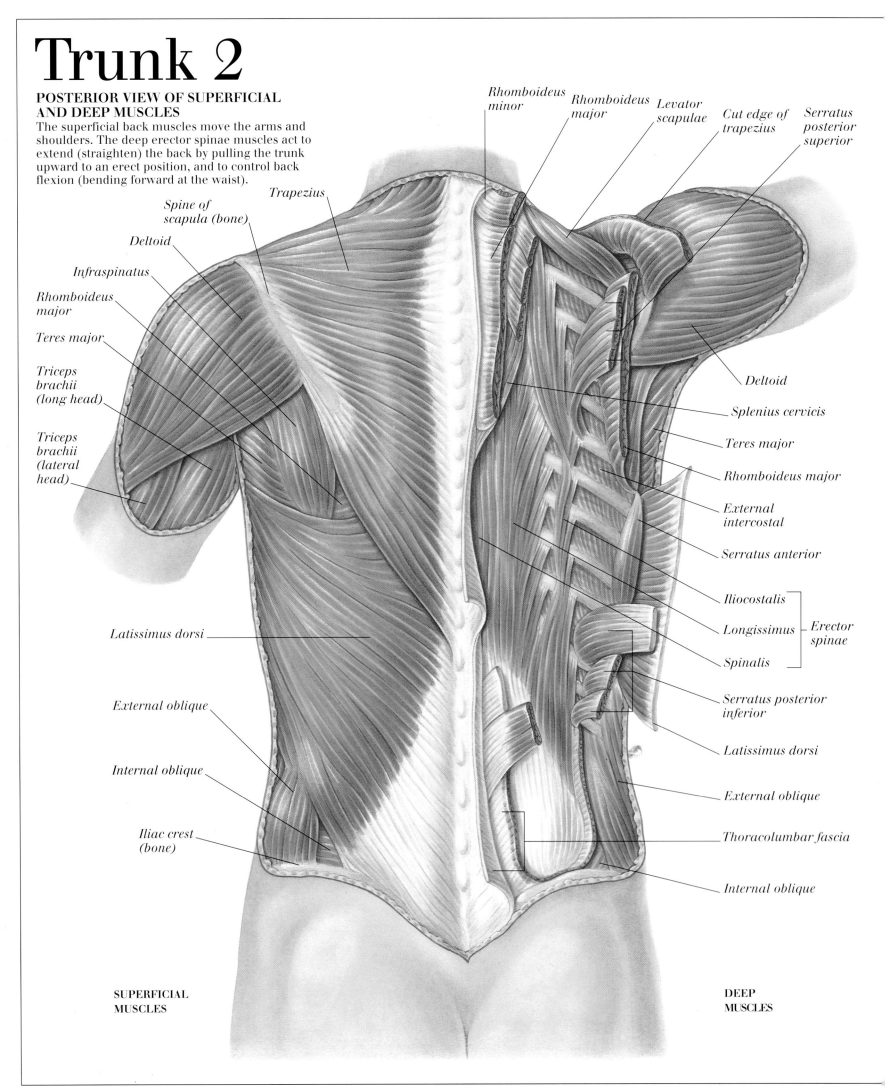

Rhomboideus minor

Rhomboideus major

Levator scapulae

Cut edge of trapezius

Serratus posterior superior

Trapezius

Spine of scapula (bone)

Deltoid

Infraspinatus

Rhomboideus major

Teres major

Triceps brachii (long head)

Triceps brachii (lateral head)

Deltoid

Splenius cervicis

Teres major

Rhomboideus major

External intercostal

Serratus anterior

Iliocostalis

Longissimus

Spinalis

Erector spinae

Latissimus dorsi

External oblique

Internal oblique

Iliac crest (bone)

Serratus posterior inferior

Latissimus dorsi

External oblique

Thoracolumbar fascia

Internal oblique

SUPERFICIAL MUSCLES

DEEP MUSCLES

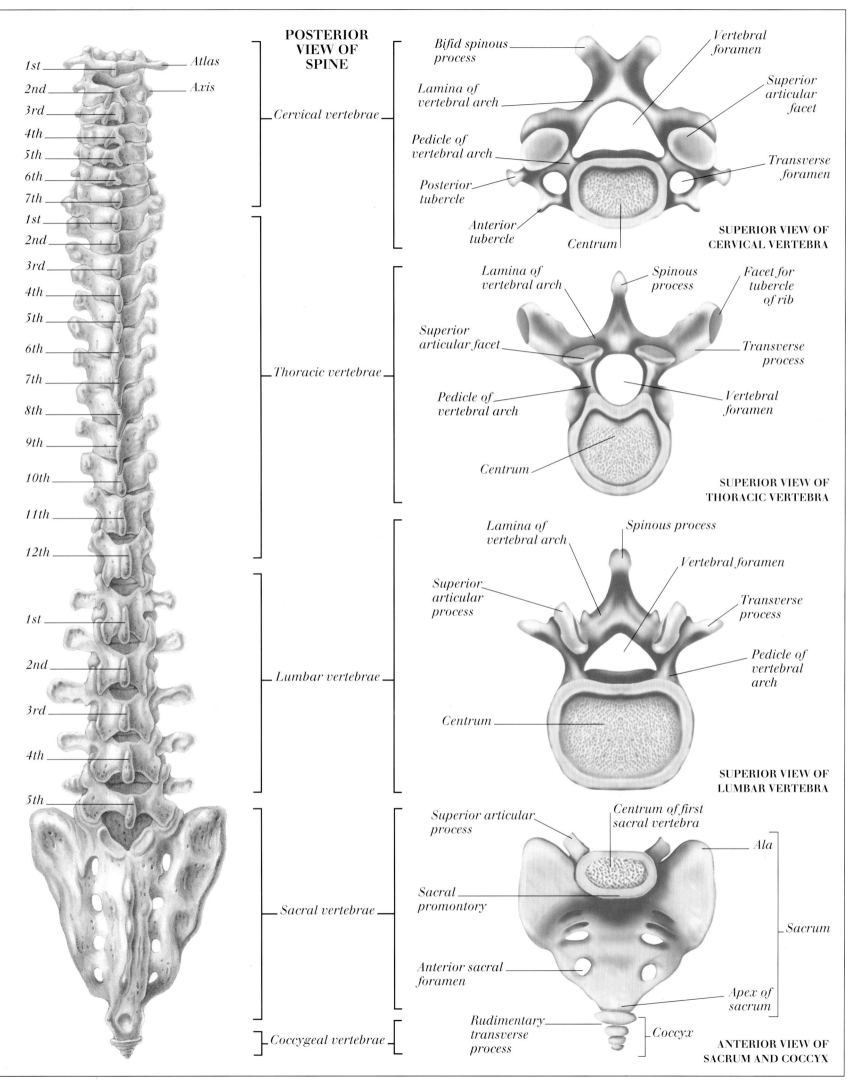

POSTERIOR VIEW OF SPINE

1st ———— *Atlas*
2nd ———— *Axis*
3rd
4th
5th
6th
7th

Cervical vertebrae

1st
2nd
3rd
4th
5th
6th
7th
8th
9th
10th
11th
12th

Thoracic vertebrae

1st
2nd
3rd
4th
5th

Lumbar vertebrae

Sacral vertebrae

Coccygeal vertebrae

Bifid spinous process
Vertebral foramen
Lamina of vertebral arch
Superior articular facet
Pedicle of vertebral arch
Transverse foramen
Posterior tubercle
Anterior tubercle
Centrum

SUPERIOR VIEW OF CERVICAL VERTEBRA

Lamina of vertebral arch
Spinous process
Facet for tubercle of rib
Superior articular facet
Transverse process
Pedicle of vertebral arch
Vertebral foramen
Centrum

SUPERIOR VIEW OF THORACIC VERTEBRA

Lamina of vertebral arch
Spinous process
Vertebral foramen
Superior articular process
Transverse process
Pedicle of vertebral arch
Centrum

SUPERIOR VIEW OF LUMBAR VERTEBRA

Superior articular process
Centrum of first sacral vertebra
Ala
Sacral promontory
Anterior sacral foramen
Sacrum
Apex of sacrum
Rudimentary transverse process
Coccyx

ANTERIOR VIEW OF SACRUM AND COCCYX

Thorax 1

THE THORAX, OR CHEST, IS THE UPPER PART OF THE TRUNK, and lies below the neck and above the abdomen. The wall of the thorax – formed by the chest muscles, ribs, and intercostal muscles – surrounds the thoracic cavity. This is separated from the abdominal cavity by the diaphragm. The thoracic cavity contains the heart and major blood vessels; right and left lungs; the trachea and bronchi; and the esophagus, which connects the throat and stomach. Two thin membranes called pleurae surround the lungs, sliding over each other to prevent friction with the thoracic wall during breathing. The heart is enclosed by membranes that form a sac called the pericardium, which protects the heart and reduces friction as it beats. Blood vessels entering the heart are the inferior and superior venae cavae and the pulmonary veins. Leaving the heart, blood is carried through the aorta and the pulmonary trunk.

THE THORACIC CAVITY

The open thorax reveals the rib cage and diaphragm, which form the boundaries of the thoracic cavity, and the heart, lungs, and major blood vessels, which occupy most of the space within the cavity.

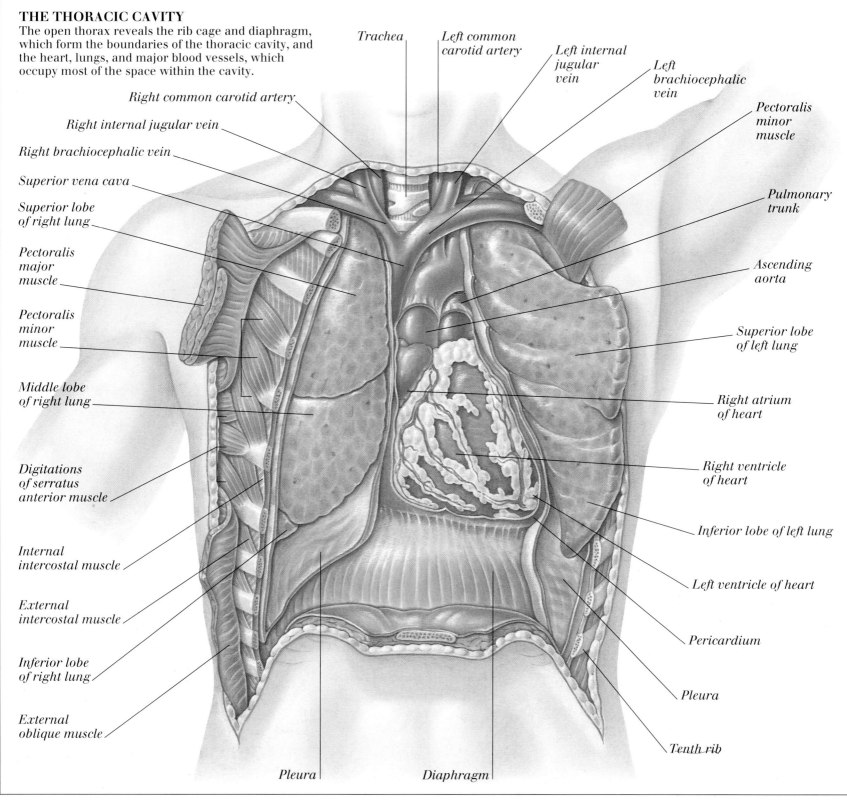

Trachea

Left common carotid artery

Left internal jugular vein

Left brachiocephalic vein

Right common carotid artery

Pectoralis minor muscle

Right internal jugular vein

Right brachiocephalic vein

Superior vena cava

Pulmonary trunk

Superior lobe of right lung

Pectoralis major muscle

Ascending aorta

Pectoralis minor muscle

Superior lobe of left lung

Middle lobe of right lung

Right atrium of heart

Digitations of serratus anterior muscle

Right ventricle of heart

Internal intercostal muscle

Inferior lobe of left lung

External intercostal muscle

Left ventricle of heart

Inferior lobe of right lung

Pericardium

External oblique muscle

Pleura

Tenth rib

Pleura

Diaphragm

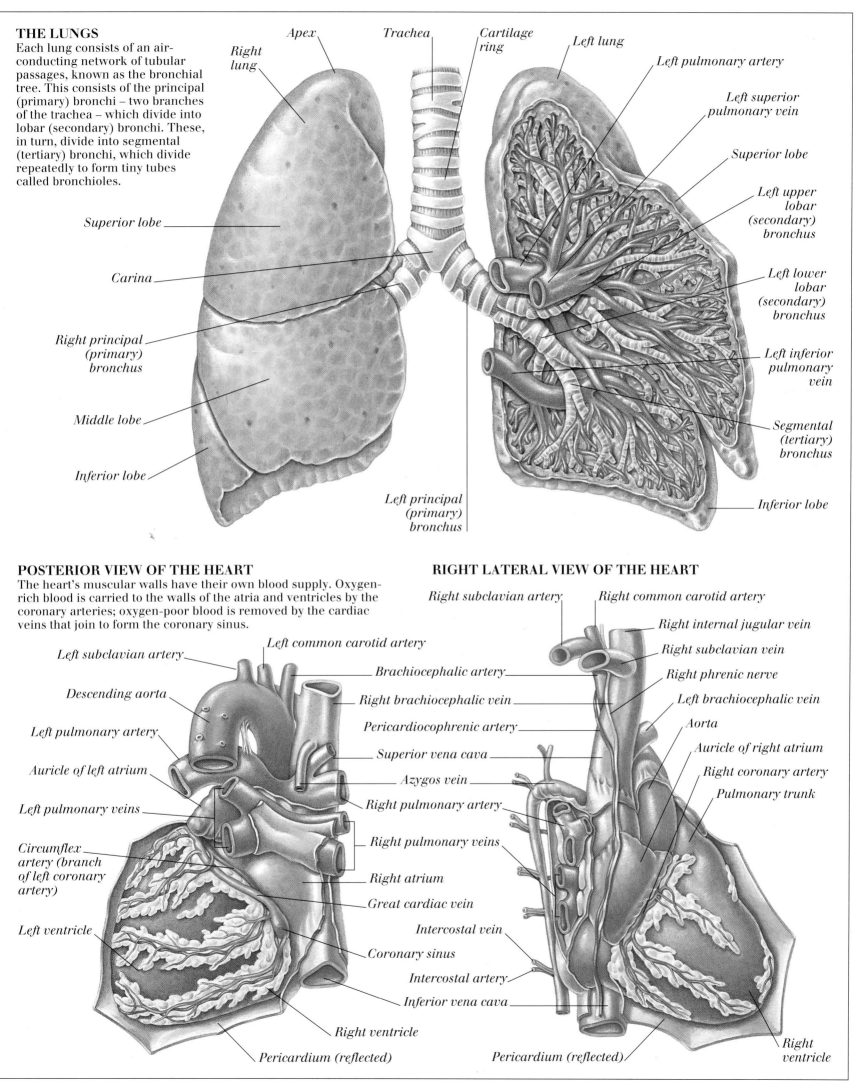

THE LUNGS
Each lung consists of an air-conducting network of tubular passages, known as the bronchial tree. This consists of the principal (primary) bronchi – two branches of the trachea – which divide into lobar (secondary) bronchi. These, in turn, divide into segmental (tertiary) bronchi, which divide repeatedly to form tiny tubes called bronchioles.

Apex

Trachea

Cartilage ring

Left lung

Left pulmonary artery

Right lung

Left superior pulmonary vein

Superior lobe

Superior lobe

Left upper lobar (secondary) bronchus

Carina

Left lower lobar (secondary) bronchus

Right principal (primary) bronchus

Left inferior pulmonary vein

Middle lobe

Segmental (tertiary) bronchus

Inferior lobe

Inferior lobe

Left principal (primary) bronchus

POSTERIOR VIEW OF THE HEART
The heart's muscular walls have their own blood supply. Oxygen-rich blood is carried to the walls of the atria and ventricles by the coronary arteries; oxygen-poor blood is removed by the cardiac veins that join to form the coronary sinus.

RIGHT LATERAL VIEW OF THE HEART

Right subclavian artery

Right common carotid artery

Left subclavian artery

Left common carotid artery

Right internal jugular vein

Descending aorta

Brachiocephalic artery

Right subclavian vein

Left pulmonary artery

Right brachiocephalic vein

Right phrenic nerve

Auricle of left atrium

Pericardiocophrenic artery

Left brachiocephalic vein

Superior vena cava

Aorta

Left pulmonary veins

Azygos vein

Auricle of right atrium

Right pulmonary artery

Right coronary artery

Circumflex artery (branch of left coronary artery)

Right pulmonary veins

Pulmonary trunk

Right atrium

Left ventricle

Great cardiac vein

Intercostal vein

Coronary sinus

Intercostal artery

Inferior vena cava

Right ventricle

Pericardium (reflected)

Right ventricle

Pericardium (reflected)

Thorax 2

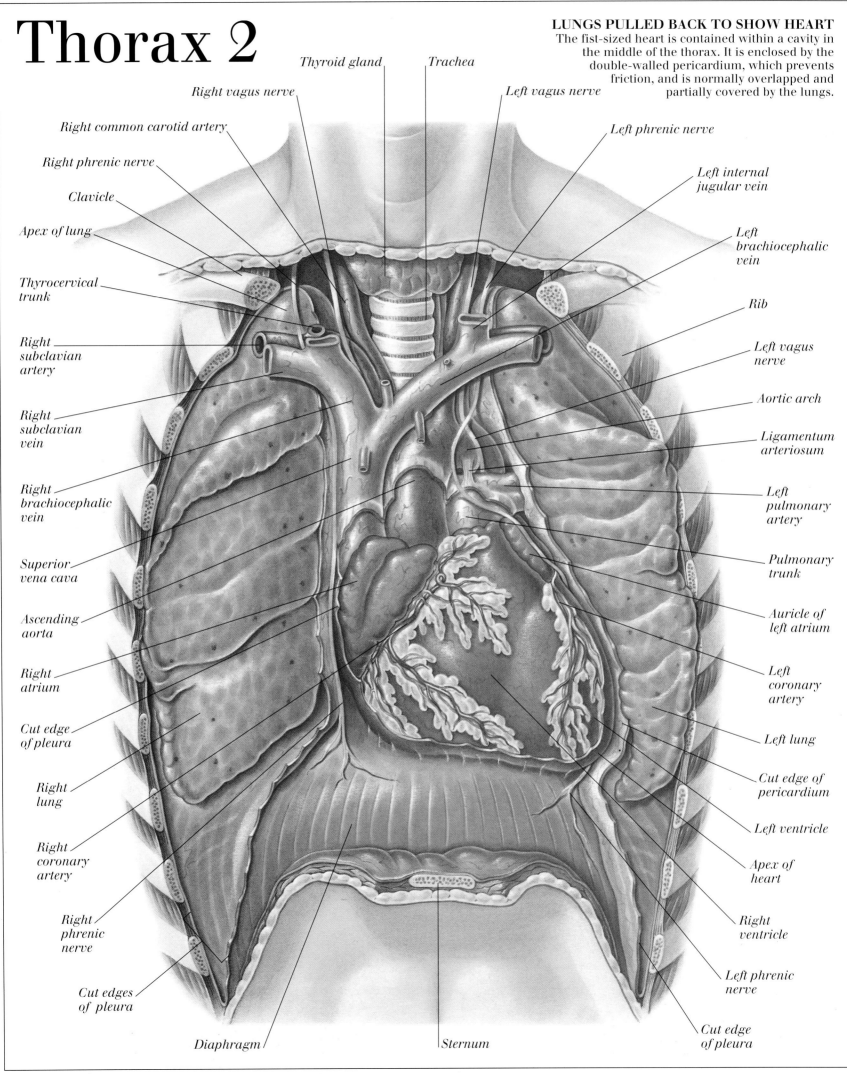

Thyroid gland

Trachea

Right vagus nerve

Left vagus nerve

Right common carotid artery

Left phrenic nerve

Right phrenic nerve

Left internal jugular vein

Clavicle

Apex of lung

Left brachiocephalic vein

Thyrocervical trunk

Rib

Right subclavian artery

Left vagus nerve

Aortic arch

Right subclavian vein

Ligamentum arteriosum

Right brachiocephalic vein

Left pulmonary artery

Superior vena cava

Pulmonary trunk

Ascending aorta

Auricle of left atrium

Right atrium

Left coronary artery

Cut edge of pleura

Left lung

Right lung

Cut edge of pericardium

Right coronary artery

Left ventricle

Apex of heart

Right phrenic nerve

Right ventricle

Cut edges of pleura

Left phrenic nerve

Diaphragm

Sternum

Cut edge of pleura

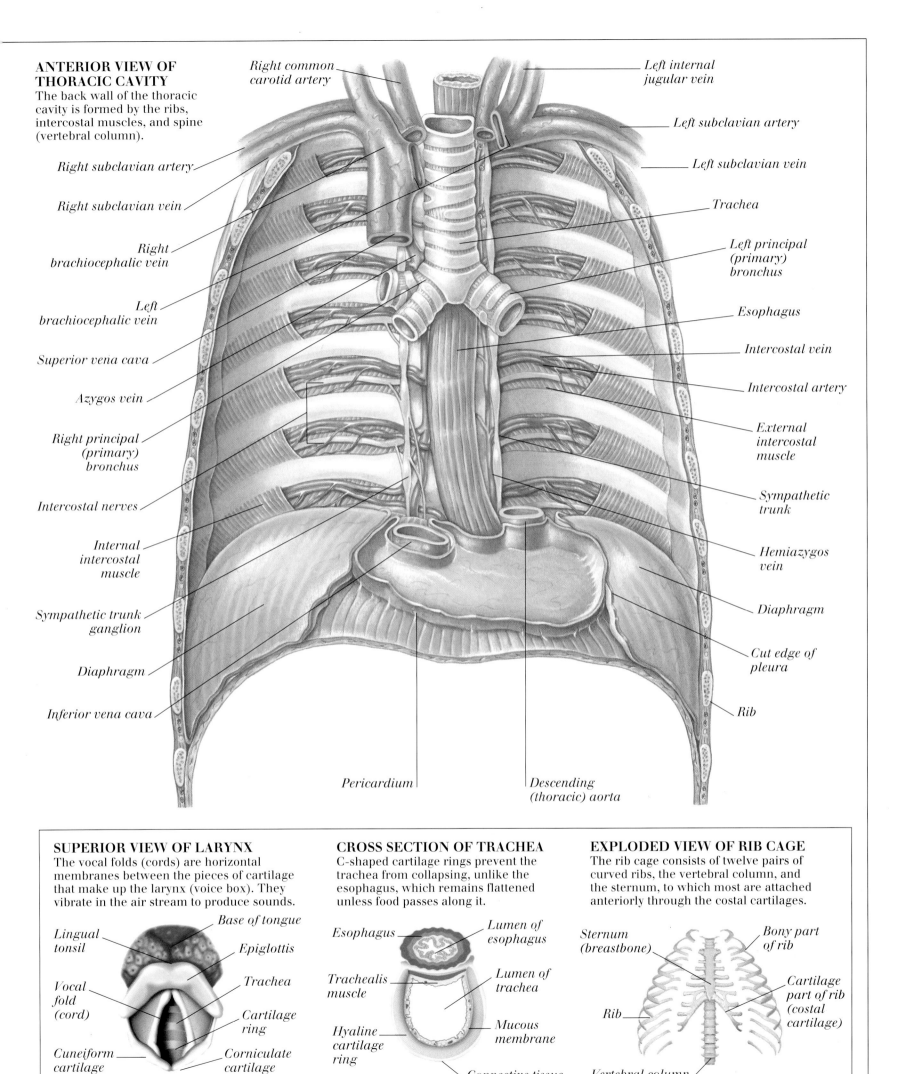

ANTERIOR VIEW OF THORACIC CAVITY

The back wall of the thoracic cavity is formed by the ribs, intercostal muscles, and spine (vertebral column).

Right common carotid artery

Left internal jugular vein

Right subclavian artery

Left subclavian artery

Right subclavian vein

Left subclavian vein

Right brachiocephalic vein

Trachea

Left principal (primary) bronchus

Left brachiocephalic vein

Esophagus

Superior vena cava

Intercostal vein

Azygos vein

Intercostal artery

Right principal (primary) bronchus

External intercostal muscle

Intercostal nerves

Sympathetic trunk

Internal intercostal muscle

Hemiazygos vein

Sympathetic trunk ganglion

Diaphragm

Diaphragm

Cut edge of pleura

Inferior vena cava

Rib

Pericardium

Descending (thoracic) aorta

SUPERIOR VIEW OF LARYNX

The vocal folds (cords) are horizontal membranes between the pieces of cartilage that make up the larynx (voice box). They vibrate in the air stream to produce sounds.

Lingual tonsil

Base of tongue

Epiglottis

Vocal fold (cord)

Trachea

Cuneiform cartilage

Cartilage ring

Corniculate cartilage

CROSS SECTION OF TRACHEA

C-shaped cartilage rings prevent the trachea from collapsing, unlike the esophagus, which remains flattened unless food passes along it.

Esophagus

Lumen of esophagus

Trachealis muscle

Lumen of trachea

Hyaline cartilage ring

Mucous membrane

Connective tissue

EXPLODED VIEW OF RIB CAGE

The rib cage consists of twelve pairs of curved ribs, the vertebral column, and the sternum, to which most are attached anteriorly through the costal cartilages.

Sternum (breastbone)

Bony part of rib

Cartilage part of rib (costal cartilage)

Rib

Vertebral column

Abdomen 1

THE ABDOMEN LIES IN THE LOWER part of the trunk between the thorax and the pelvis. The wall of the abdomen surrounds the abdominal cavity (which is separated from the thoracic cavity by the diaphragm), and protects the organs contained within it. Four pairs of muscles form the abdominal wall: the external oblique, internal oblique, transversus abdominis, and rectus abdominis. Within the abdominal cavity are the stomach and the small and large intestines, which are all digestive organs; the liver and pancreas, which are associated with the digestive system; the spleen, which forms part of the body's defenses against disease; and two kidneys, which remove waste products from the blood. A thin, continuous membrane called the peritoneum covers the abdominal organs and lines the abdominal cavity to prevent organs from sticking to each other and causing severe pain. In the lower abdomen, the dorsal aorta (the large artery that carries blood away from the heart) divides into right and left common iliac arteries, which supply the pelvic region and legs. The right and left common iliac veins join to form the inferior vena cava, a large vein that carries blood back to the heart.

THE GALLBLADDER
This muscular sac stores a greenish liquid called bile, produced by the liver. During digestion, the gallbladder contracts, squirting bile along ducts into the duodenum, where it aids the breakdown of fats.

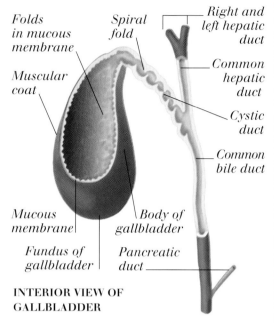

Folds in mucous membrane

Spiral fold

Right and left hepatic duct

Muscular coat

Common hepatic duct

Cystic duct

Common bile duct

Mucous membrane

Body of gallbladder

Fundus of gallbladder

Pancreatic duct

INTERIOR VIEW OF GALLBLADDER

SUPERFICIAL VIEW OF ABDOMINAL CAVITY
The greater omentum covers the intestines like a fatty apron. It serves to attach digestive organs to each other and to the body wall, and to protect and insulate the intestines.

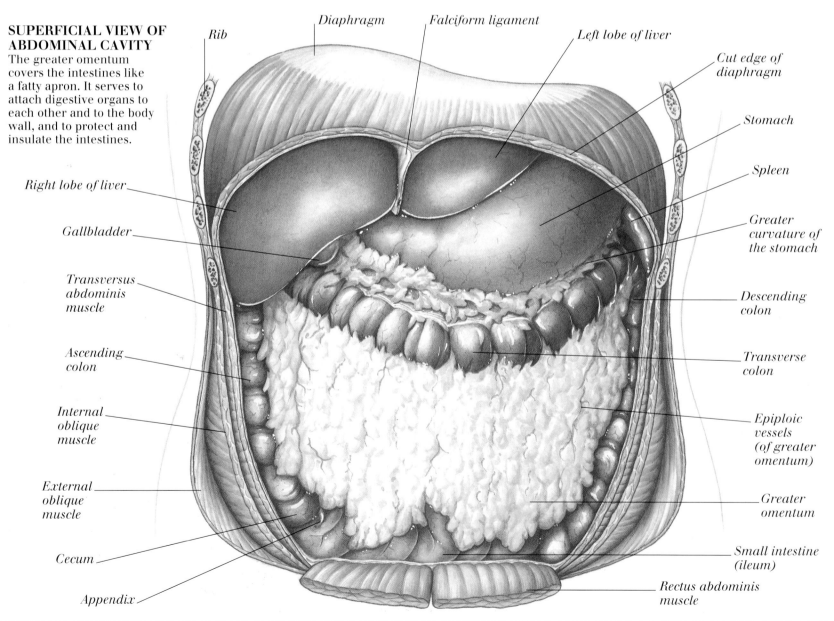

Diaphragm

Rib

Falciform ligament

Left lobe of liver

Cut edge of diaphragm

Stomach

Spleen

Greater curvature of the stomach

Right lobe of liver

Gallbladder

Transversus abdominis muscle

Ascending colon

Internal oblique muscle

External oblique muscle

Cecum

Appendix

Descending colon

Transverse colon

Epiploic vessels (of greater omentum)

Greater omentum

Small intestine (ileum)

Rectus abdominis muscle

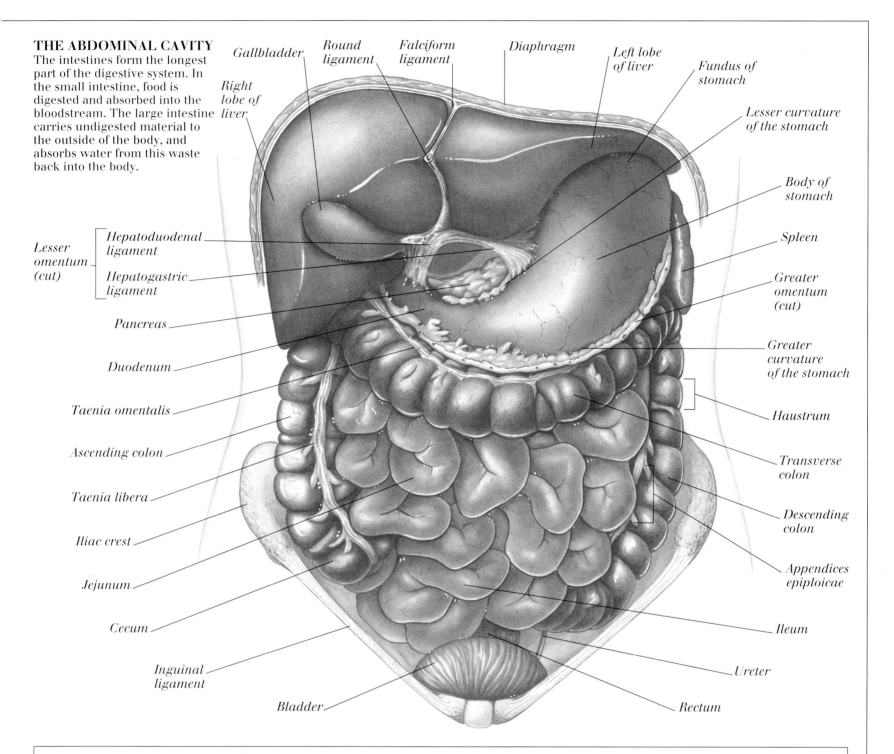

THE ABDOMINAL CAVITY

The intestines form the longest part of the digestive system. In the small intestine, food is digested and absorbed into the bloodstream. The large intestine carries undigested material to the outside of the body, and absorbs water from this waste back into the body.

Gallbladder

Round ligament

Falciform ligament

Diaphragm

Left lobe of liver

Fundus of stomach

Right lobe of liver

Lesser curvature of the stomach

Body of stomach

Lesser omentum (cut)

Hepatoduodenal ligament

Hepatogastric ligament

Spleen

Greater omentum (cut)

Pancreas

Greater curvature of the stomach

Duodenum

Taenia omentalis

Haustrum

Ascending colon

Taenia libera

Transverse colon

Iliac crest

Descending colon

Jejunum

Appendices epiploicae

Cecum

Ileum

Inguinal ligament

Ureter

Bladder

Rectum

THE LIVER

The liver is the body's largest gland. It performs over 500 functions, which include processing the blood that arrives through the hepatic portal vein, its direct link with the digestive system (see pp. 22-23), and the hepatic artery. It controls levels of fats, amino acids, and glucose in the blood; stores vitamins A and D; removes worn-out red blood cells; removes drugs and poisons; warms the blood; and produces bile, which is used in digestion. Blood leaves the liver through the hepatic veins, which empty into the inferior vena cava.

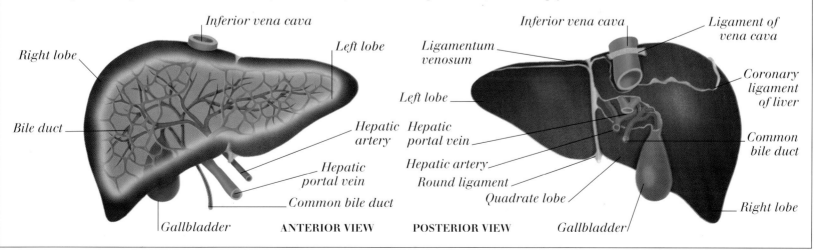

Inferior vena cava

Left lobe

Right lobe

Bile duct

Hepatic artery

Hepatic portal vein

Common bile duct

Gallbladder

ANTERIOR VIEW

Inferior vena cava

Ligament of vena cava

Ligamentum venosum

Left lobe

Coronary ligament of liver

Hepatic portal vein

Hepatic artery

Round ligament

Common bile duct

Quadrate lobe

Gallbladder

Right lobe

POSTERIOR VIEW

Abdomen 2

The removal of the liver reveals the opening in the diaphragm through which the esophagus enters the abdomen from the thorax. The esophagus carries food into the stomach and then the duodenum, which is the first, short section of the small intestine.

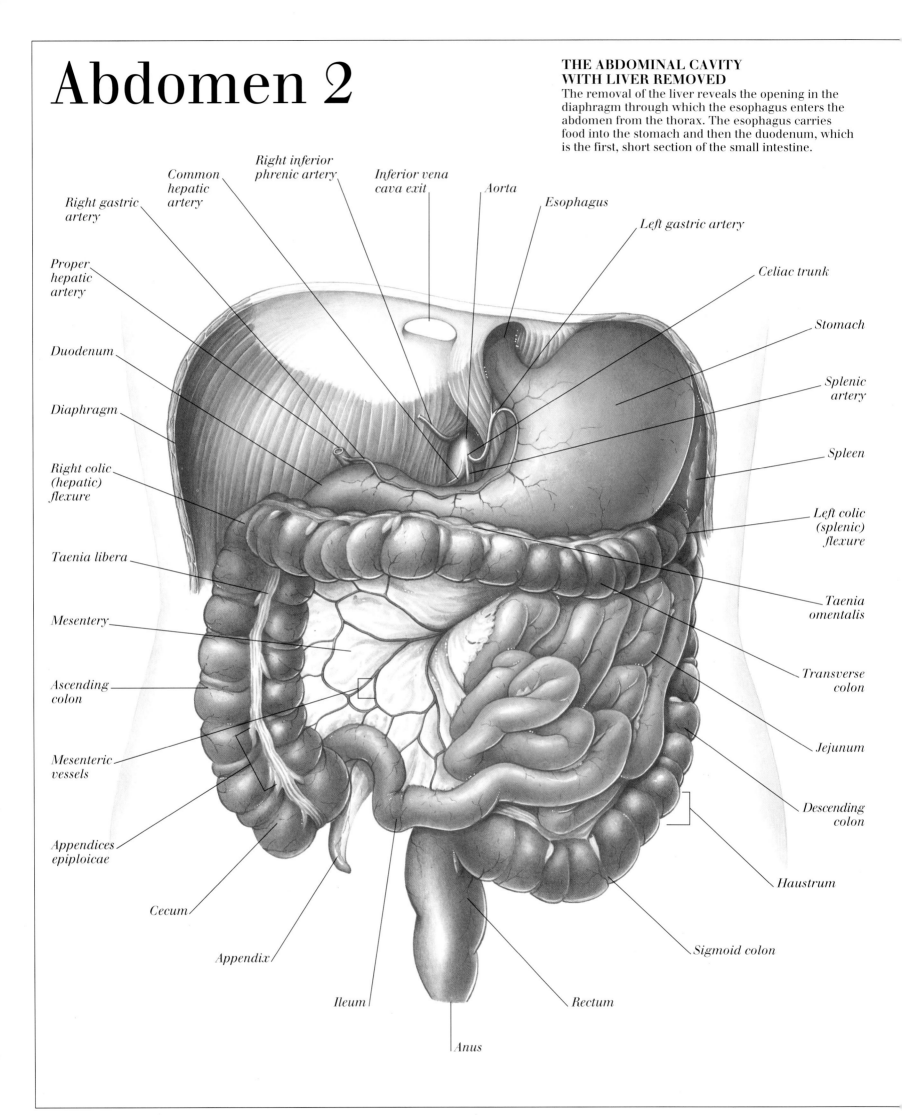

Right gastric artery

Common hepatic artery

Right inferior phrenic artery

Inferior vena cava exit

Aorta

Esophagus

Left gastric artery

Celiac trunk

Proper hepatic artery

Stomach

Duodenum

Splenic artery

Diaphragm

Spleen

Right colic (hepatic) flexure

Left colic (splenic) flexure

Taenia libera

Taenia omentalis

Mesentery

Ascending colon

Transverse colon

Mesenteric vessels

Jejunum

Descending colon

Appendices epiploicae

Haustrum

Cecum

Sigmoid colon

Appendix

Ileum

Rectum

Anus

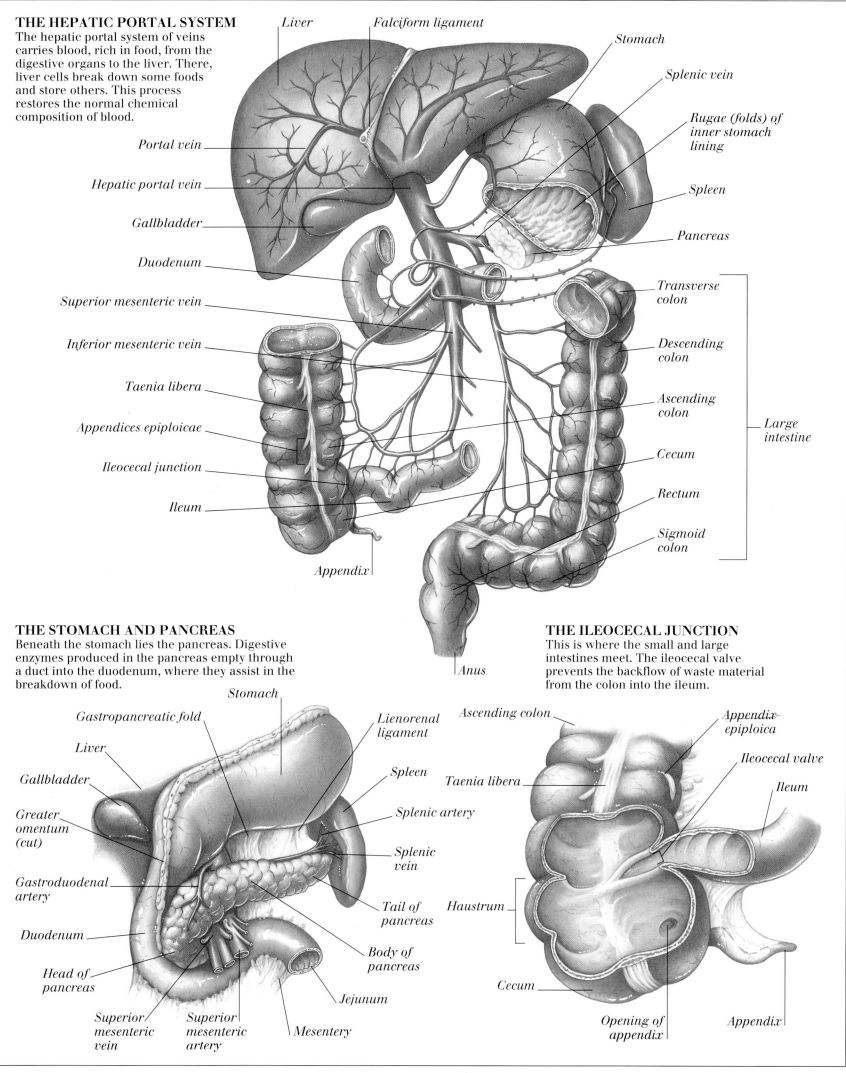

THE HEPATIC PORTAL SYSTEM
The hepatic portal system of veins carries blood, rich in food, from the digestive organs to the liver. There, liver cells break down some foods and store others. This process restores the normal chemical composition of blood.

Liver

Falciform ligament

Stomach

Splenic vein

Rugae (folds) of inner stomach lining

Spleen

Pancreas

Portal vein

Hepatic portal vein

Gallbladder

Duodenum

Superior mesenteric vein

Inferior mesenteric vein

Taenia libera

Appendices epiploicae

Ileocecal junction

Ileum

Appendix

Transverse colon

Descending colon

Ascending colon

Cecum

Rectum

Sigmoid colon

Large intestine

Anus

THE STOMACH AND PANCREAS
Beneath the stomach lies the pancreas. Digestive enzymes produced in the pancreas empty through a duct into the duodenum, where they assist in the breakdown of food.

Stomach

Gastropancreatic fold

Liver

Gallbladder

Greater omentum (cut)

Gastroduodenal artery

Duodenum

Head of pancreas

Superior mesenteric vein

Superior mesenteric artery

Mesentery

Jejunum

Body of pancreas

Tail of pancreas

Splenic vein

Splenic artery

Spleen

Lienorenal ligament

THE ILEOCECAL JUNCTION
This is where the small and large intestines meet. The ileocecal valve prevents the backflow of waste material from the colon into the ileum.

Ascending colon

Taenia libera

Haustrum

Cecum

Opening of appendix

Appendix

Appendix epiploica

Ileocecal valve

Ileum

Abdomen 3

The removal of the digestive organs reveals the two kidneys, which remove waste products and excess water from blood. Blood enters the kidneys through the renal arteries; the waste is then passed to the bladder, where it is stored before release from the body.

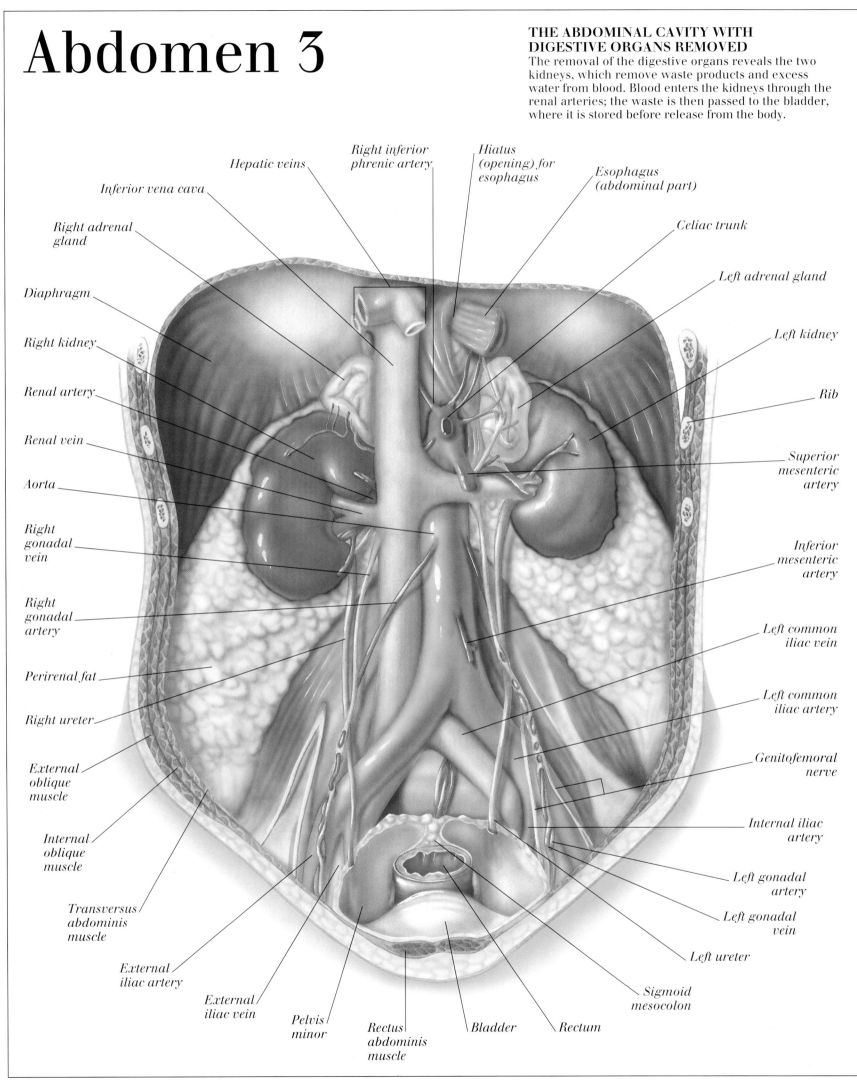

Right inferior phrenic artery

Hepatic veins

Hiatus (opening) for esophagus

Esophagus (abdominal part)

Inferior vena cava

Celiac trunk

Right adrenal gland

Left adrenal gland

Diaphragm

Left kidney

Right kidney

Rib

Renal artery

Renal vein

Superior mesenteric artery

Aorta

Right gonadal vein

Inferior mesenteric artery

Right gonadal artery

Left common iliac vein

Perirenal fat

Left common iliac artery

Right ureter

Genitofemoral nerve

External oblique muscle

Internal iliac artery

Internal oblique muscle

Left gonadal artery

Transversus abdominis muscle

Left gonadal vein

External iliac artery

Left ureter

External iliac vein

Sigmoid mesocolon

Pelvis minor

Rectus abdominis muscle

Bladder

Rectum

THE POSTERIOR ABDOMINAL WALL

Major muscles of the posterior abdominal wall include the quadratus lumborum, which helps support the backbone; the iliacus and psoas major, which flex the hip and help maintain posture; and the transversus abdominis, which compresses abdominal contents.

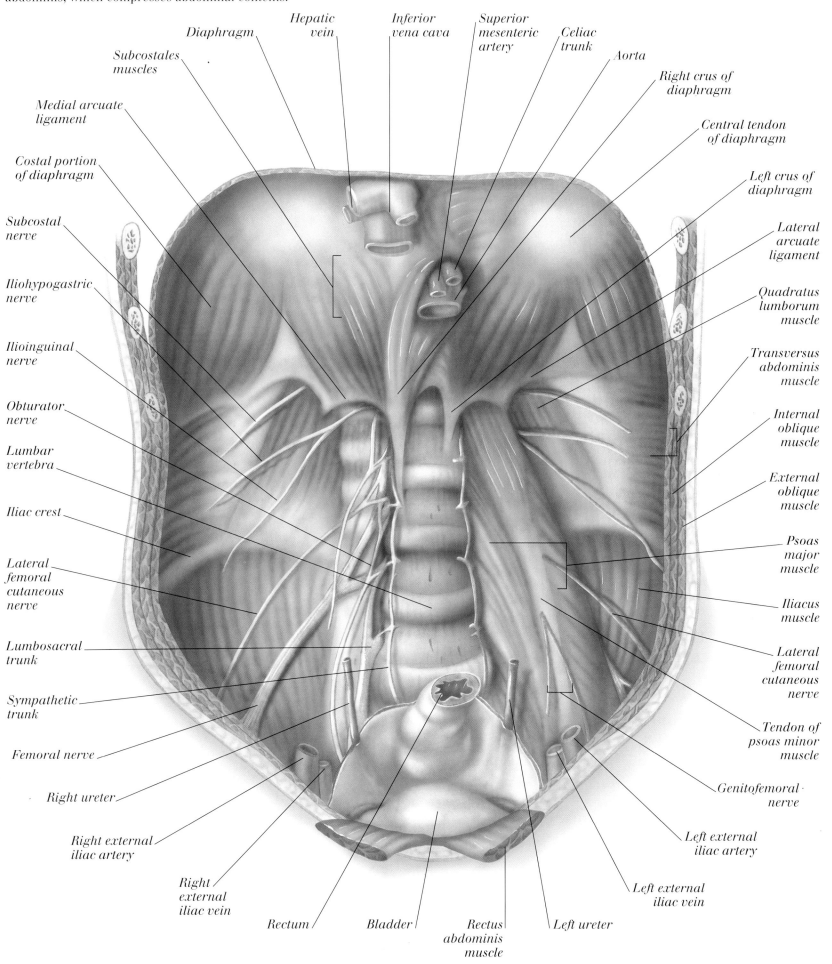

Diaphragm

Hepatic vein

Inferior vena cava

Superior mesenteric artery

Celiac trunk

Aorta

Right crus of diaphragm

Central tendon of diaphragm

Left crus of diaphragm

Lateral arcuate ligament

Quadratus lumborum muscle

Transversus abdominis muscle

Internal oblique muscle

External oblique muscle

Psoas major muscle

Iliacus muscle

Lateral femoral cutaneous nerve

Tendon of psoas minor muscle

Genitofemoral nerve

Left external iliac artery

Left external iliac vein

Subcostales muscles

Medial arcuate ligament

Costal portion of diaphragm

Subcostal nerve

Iliohypogastric nerve

Ilioinguinal nerve

Obturator nerve

Lumbar vertebra

Iliac crest

Lateral femoral cutaneous nerve

Lumbosacral trunk

Sympathetic trunk

Femoral nerve

Right ureter

Right external iliac artery

Right external iliac vein

Rectum

Bladder

Rectus abdominis muscle

Left ureter

Pelvic region 1

THE PELVIC AREA IS THE LOWEST part of the trunk. It lies below the abdomen and above the junction between the trunk and the legs. The framework of the pelvic region is formed anteriorly and laterally by the pelvic (hip) girdle, and posteriorly by the sacrum, which is part of the vertebral column. Together, these bones form the bowl-shaped pelvis, which provides attachment sites for the muscles of the legs and trunk, and surrounds and protects the organs within the pelvic cavity. The pelvic cavity is continuous with, and lies below, the abdominal cavity. It contains the rectum, the terminal region of the large intestine, which opens out of the body through the anus; the bladder, which is a muscular bag that stores urine; and the internal reproductive organs of the male and female. The muscles of the pelvic floor, or pelvic diaphragm – which include the levator ani – close the lower opening of the pelvis (the pelvic outlet) and support the pelvic organs, preventing them from being forced downward by the weight of the contents of the abdomen.

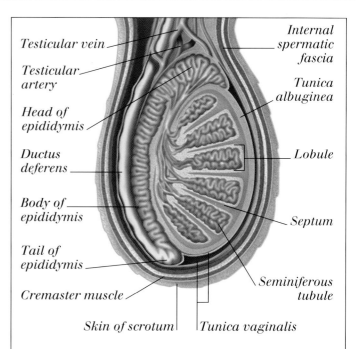

Testicular vein
Testicular artery
Head of epididymis
Ductus deferens
Body of epididymis
Tail of epididymis
Cremaster muscle
Skin of scrotum
Internal spermatic fascia
Tunica albuginea
Lobule
Septum
Seminiferous tubule
Tunica vaginalis

ANATOMY OF THE TESTIS
The testis consists of tightly coiled, sperm-producing seminiferous tubules connected through efferent ducts to the crescent-shaped epididymis. Sperm mature here before entering the ductus deferens, which carries them toward the penis.

MALE PERINEUM
The perineum overlies the pelvic floor. Its muscles include the anal sphincter, which controls the release of feces; the urogenital diaphragm, which controls the release of urine; the bulbospongiosus, which empties the urethra of urine; and the ischiocavernosus, which helps maintain penile erection.

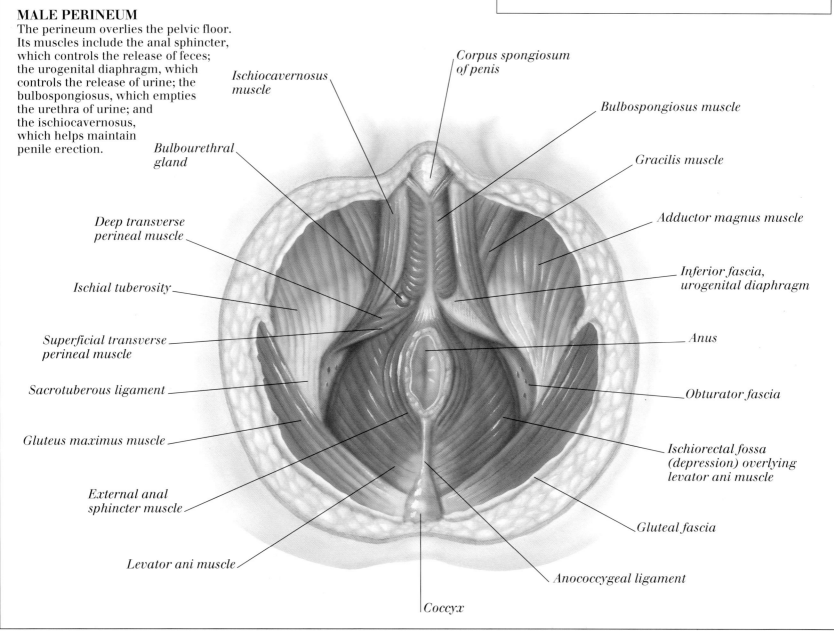

Ischiocavernosus muscle
Corpus spongiosum of penis
Bulbospongiosus muscle
Gracilis muscle
Bulbourethral gland
Adductor magnus muscle
Deep transverse perineal muscle
Inferior fascia, urogenital diaphragm
Ischial tuberosity
Anus
Superficial transverse perineal muscle
Sacrotuberous ligament
Obturator fascia
Gluteus maximus muscle
Ischiorectal fossa (depression) overlying levator ani muscle
External anal sphincter muscle
Gluteal fascia
Levator ani muscle
Anococcygeal ligament
Coccyx

MALE PELVIC CAVITY

Most of the male reproductive system lies outside the pelvic cavity. From each of the testes runs a ductus deferens that joins the urethra in the prostate gland. The urethra opens through the erectile penis.

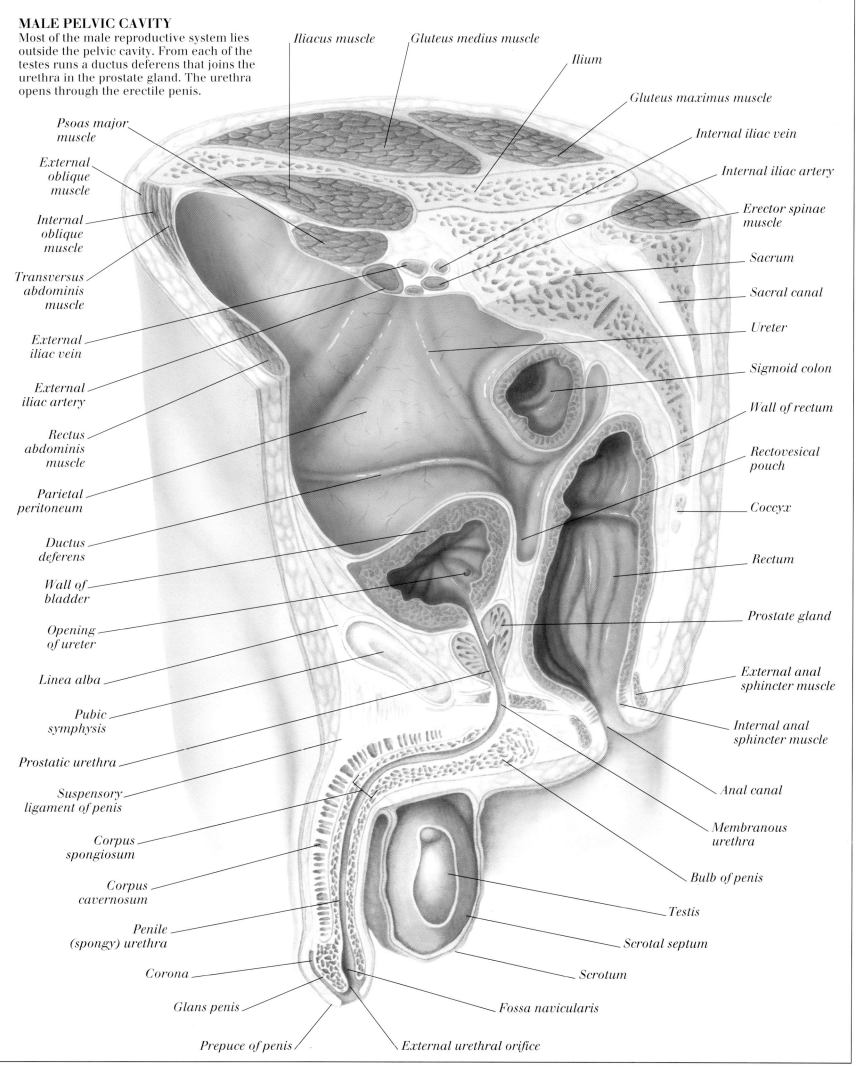

Iliacus muscle

Gluteus medius muscle

Ilium

Gluteus maximus muscle

Internal iliac vein

Internal iliac artery

Erector spinae muscle

Sacrum

Sacral canal

Ureter

Sigmoid colon

Wall of rectum

Rectovesical pouch

Coccyx

Rectum

Prostate gland

External anal sphincter muscle

Internal anal sphincter muscle

Anal canal

Membranous urethra

Bulb of penis

Testis

Scrotal septum

Scrotum

Fossa navicularis

External urethral orifice

Psoas major muscle

External oblique muscle

Internal oblique muscle

Transversus abdominis muscle

External iliac vein

External iliac artery

Rectus abdominis muscle

Parietal peritoneum

Ductus deferens

Wall of bladder

Opening of ureter

Linea alba

Pubic symphysis

Prostatic urethra

Suspensory ligament of penis

Corpus spongiosum

Corpus cavernosum

Penile (spongy) urethra

Corona

Glans penis

Prepuce of penis

Pelvic region 2

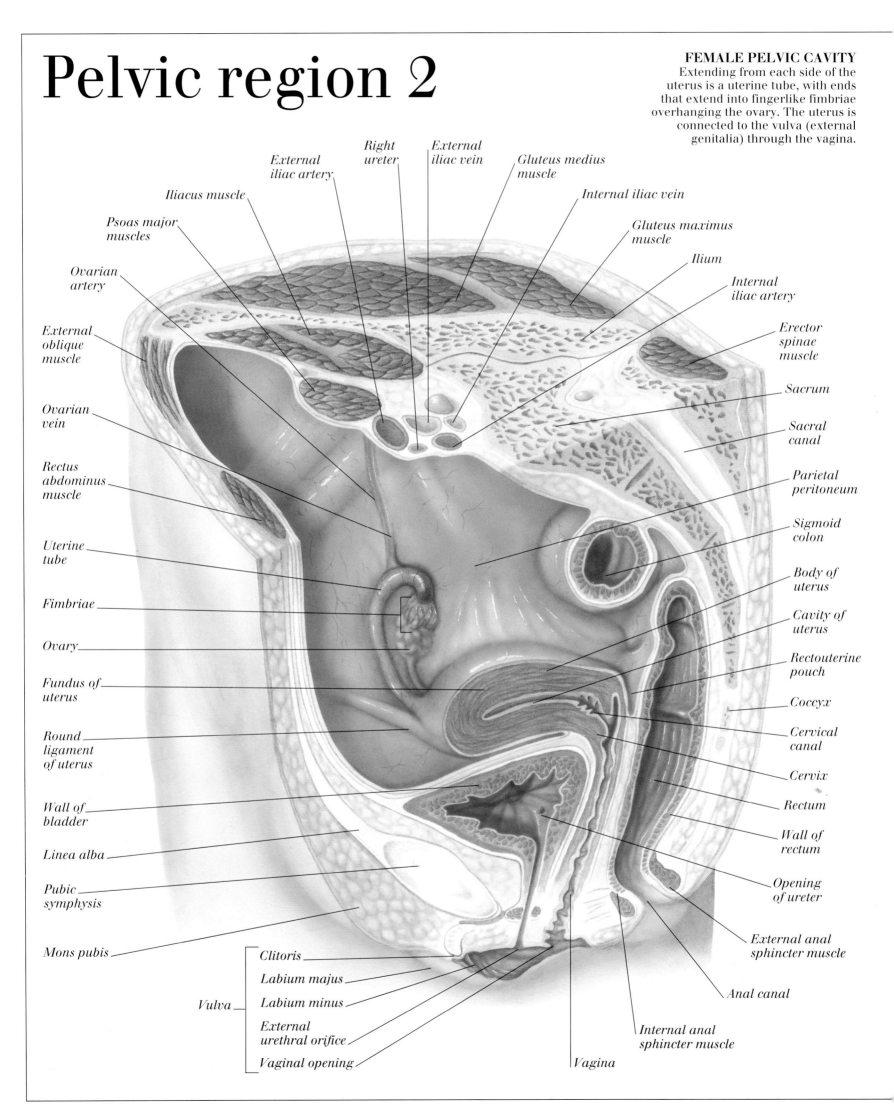

External
iliac artery

Right
ureter

External
iliac vein

Gluteus medius
muscle

Iliacus muscle

Internal iliac vein

Psoas major
muscles

Gluteus maximus
muscle

Ovarian
artery

Ilium

Internal
iliac artery

External
oblique
muscle

Erector
spinae
muscle

Ovarian
vein

Sacrum

Rectus
abdominus
muscle

Sacral
canal

Parietal
peritoneum

Uterine
tube

Sigmoid
colon

Fimbriae

Body of
uterus

Ovary

Cavity of
uterus

Fundus of
uterus

Rectouterine
pouch

Coccyx

Round
ligament
of uterus

Cervical
canal

Cervix

Wall of
bladder

Rectum

Linea alba

Wall of
rectum

Pubic
symphysis

Opening
of ureter

Mons pubis

External anal
sphincter muscle

Clitoris

Labium majus

Anal canal

Vulva

Labium minus

External
urethral orifice

Internal anal
sphincter muscle

Vaginal opening

Vagina

THE MENSTRUAL CYCLE

Throughout every month, women of reproductive age experience the menstrual cycle – a sequence of events that prepares their bodies for pregnancy. It has three phases. During the menstrual phase (also known as the "period"), the lining of the uterus breaks down, and is shed with some blood through the vagina. The proliferative phase, when the uterine lining thickens once more, coincides with the ripening of a new egg (ovum) inside the ovary. After the egg is released at ovulation, around day 14, the uterine lining thickens still further during the secretory phase, in readiness to receive the egg, should it be fertilized by a sperm. If the egg is not fertilized, and there is no pregnancy, the uterine lining breaks down and is shed, and the cycle begins again.

MENSTRUAL (DAYS 1–5)

Uterine tube

Ovary

Uterus

Cervix

Vagina

The uterine lining and blood are shed through the vagina

PROLIFERATIVE (DAYS 6–14)

New egg matures and is released into uterine tube (ovulation)

Endometrium (lining of uterus) thickens

Endometrium thickens but eventually breaks down if egg remains unfertilized

SECRETORY (DAYS 15–28)

Egg travels along the uterine tube into the uterus

FEMALE PERINEUM

The urinogenital diaphragm and the anal sphincter control the release of urine and feces respectively. The bulbospongiosus constricts the vaginal opening; the ischiocavernosus assists in erection of the clitoris.

Mons pubis

Labium minus

Gracilis muscle

Vaginal opening

Ischiocavernosus muscle

Adductor magnus muscle

Deep transverse perineal muscle

Sacrotuberous ligament

Ischiorectal fossa

Gluteus maximus muscle

Gluteal fascia

Anococcygeal ligament

Glans clitoris

Prepuce of clitoris

External urethra orifice

Wall of vagina

Bulbospongiosus muscle

Superficial transverse perineal muscle

Ischial tuberosity

External anal sphincter muscle

Obturator fascia

Anus

Levator ani muscle

Coccyx

Shoulder and upper arm

THE BONY FRAMEWORK OF THE SHOULDER and upper arm is formed by the scapula (shoulder blade), clavicle (collarbone), and humerus (upper arm bone). At its upper end, the humerus forms a joint with the scapula at the shoulder, which permits movement of the upper arm in all planes. The group of muscles that cross the shoulder joint to move the humerus include the deltoid, pectoralis major, latissimus dorsi, and teres major. The supraspinatus, infraspinatus, teres minor, and subscapularis – collectively, the rotator cuff muscles – stabilize the shoulder joint, preventing its dislocation. At its lower end, the humerus forms a joint with the radius and ulna (forearm bones) at the elbow, which permits flexion (bending) and extension (straightening) only. The muscles that flex the elbow include the biceps brachii, brachioradialis, and brachialis; the muscle that extends the elbow is the triceps brachii. Blood is carried into the arm by the axillary artery (which becomes the brachial artery as it enters the upper arm), and out of the arm by the cephalic vein and the brachial and basilic veins (which join to form the axillary vein as they enter the shoulder). The main nerves supplying the upper arm include the radial, median, and ulnar nerves.

ANTERIOR VIEW OF SUPERFICIAL MUSCLES
The major anterior superficial muscles are the deltoid and pectoralis major, which pull the arm forward or backward, and the biceps ("two heads") brachii, which flexes the arm at the elbow.

ANTERIOR VIEW OF DEEP MUSCLES
The removal of superficial muscles reveals the coracobrachialis muscle. This pulls the arm forward and upward, or toward the body.

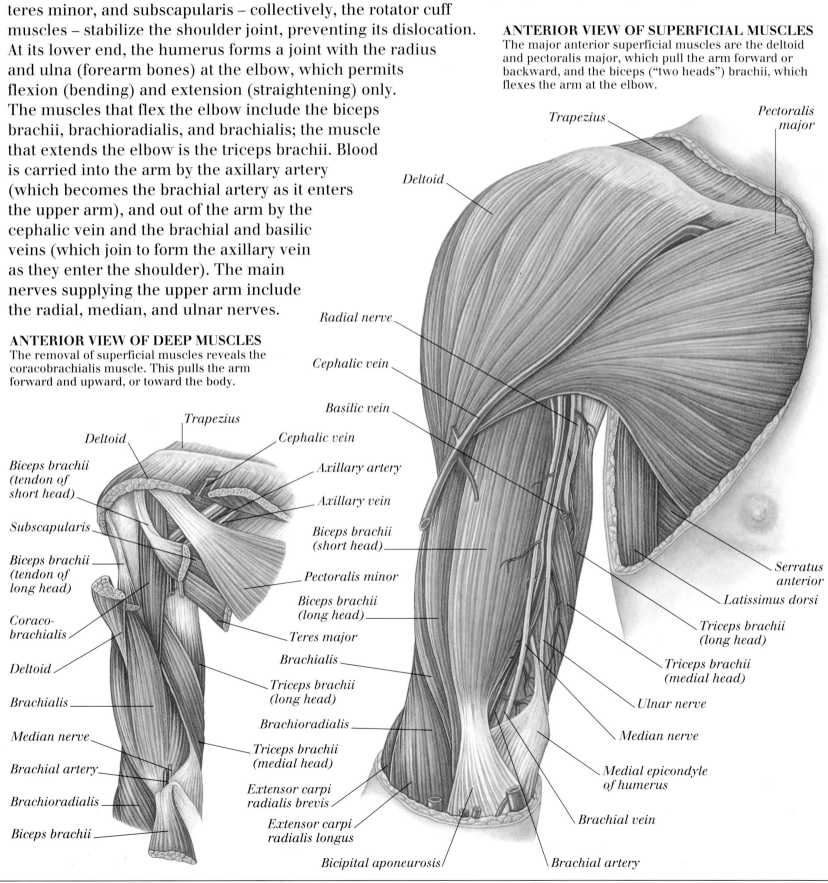

52

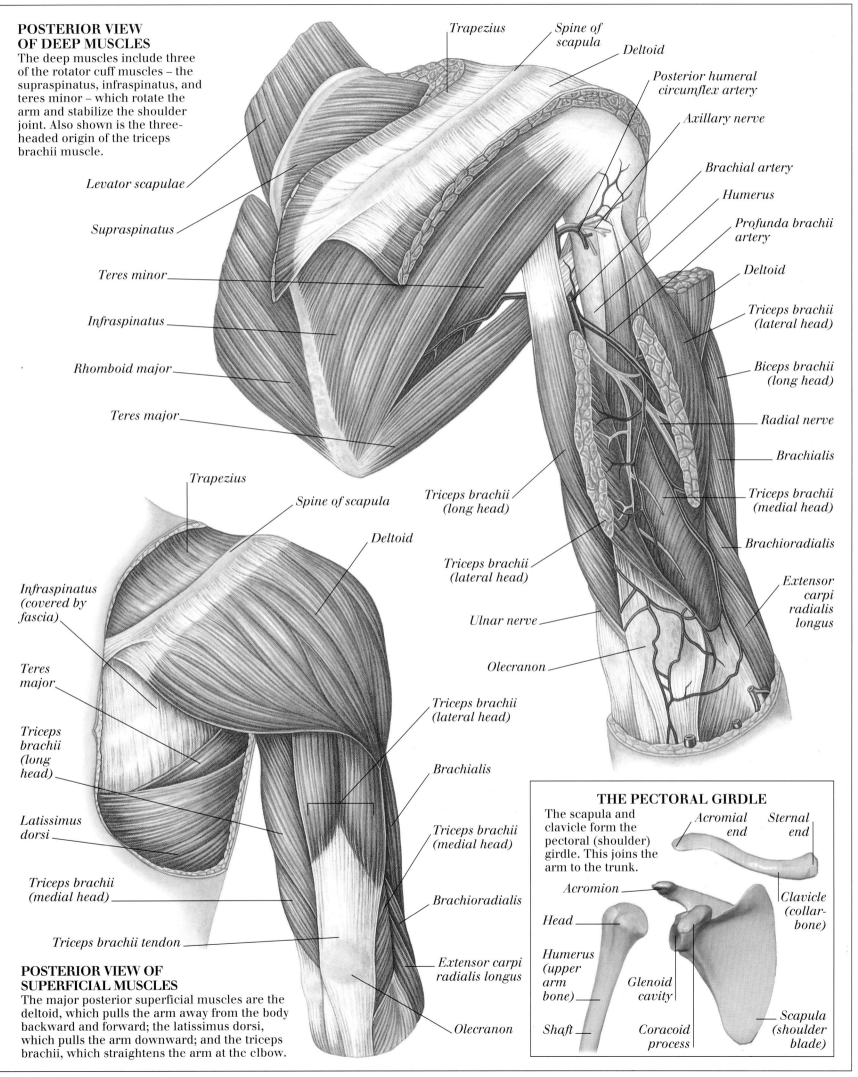

POSTERIOR VIEW OF DEEP MUSCLES

The deep muscles include three of the rotator cuff muscles – the supraspinatus, infraspinatus, and teres minor – which rotate the arm and stabilize the shoulder joint. Also shown is the three-headed origin of the triceps brachii muscle.

Levator scapulae

Supraspinatus

Teres minor

Infraspinatus

Rhomboid major

Teres major

Trapezius

Spine of scapula

Deltoid

Posterior humeral circumflex artery

Axillary nerve

Brachial artery

Humerus

Profunda brachii artery

Deltoid

Triceps brachii (lateral head)

Biceps brachii (long head)

Radial nerve

Brachialis

Triceps brachii (medial head)

Brachioradialis

Extensor carpi radialis longus

Triceps brachii (long head)

Triceps brachii (lateral head)

Ulnar nerve

Olecranon

Trapezius

Spine of scapula

Deltoid

Infraspinatus (covered by fascia)

Teres major

Triceps brachii (long head)

Latissimus dorsi

Triceps brachii (medial head)

Triceps brachii tendon

Brachialis

Triceps brachii (medial head)

Brachioradialis

Extensor carpi radialis longus

Olecranon

POSTERIOR VIEW OF SUPERFICIAL MUSCLES

The major posterior superficial muscles are the deltoid, which pulls the arm away from the body backward and forward; the latissimus dorsi, which pulls the arm downward; and the triceps brachii, which straightens the arm at the elbow.

THE PECTORAL GIRDLE

The scapula and clavicle form the pectoral (shoulder) girdle. This joins the arm to the trunk.

Acromial end

Sternal end

Acromion

Head

Humerus (upper arm bone)

Shaft

Glenoid cavity

Coracoid process

Clavicle (collarbone)

Scapula (shoulder blade)

Forearm and hand

THE HAND IS CAPABLE OF A WIDE range of precise movements. It owes its flexibility and versatility to the many muscles of the forearm and hand, and to a bony framework that consists of fourteen phalanges (finger bones), five metacarpals (palm bones), and eight carpals (wrist bones), four of which articulate with the ends of the radius and ulna (forearm bones) at the wrist joint. Forearm muscles taper into long tendons that extend into the hand. These tendons, along with blood vessels and nerves, are held in place by two fibrous bands: the flexor retinaculum and the extensor retinaculum. Most muscles in the anterior (inner) part of the forearm are flexors; most in the posterior (outer) part are extensors. Wrist flexors include the flexor carpi radialis; wrist extensors include the extensor carpi ulnaris. Finger flexors include the flexor digitorum superficialis; finger extensors include the extensor digitorum. Inside the hand, the lumbrical and the interosseus muscles between the metacarpals flex the metacarpophalangeal (knuckle) joints and extend the fingers.

SUPERIOR VIEW OF BONES OF THE HAND
The long phalanges, which shape the fingers of the hand, together with the bones of the metacarpus (palm) and carpus (wrist), enable the hand to perform gripping movements. These range from the precision grip used when holding a pen to the power grip used when making a fist.

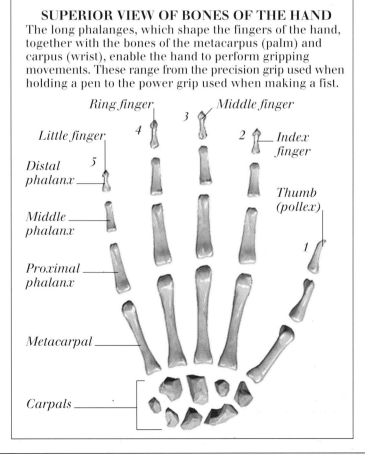

Ring finger
Middle finger
Little finger
4
3
Index finger
2
Distal phalanx
5
Thumb (pollex)
Middle phalanx
1
Proximal phalanx
Metacarpal
Carpals

ANTERIOR VIEW OF SUPERFICIAL MUSCLES
The median nerve controls the action of most of the flexor muscles of the forearm, which flex the wrist, and the flexor and abductor pollicis brevis, which move the thumb.

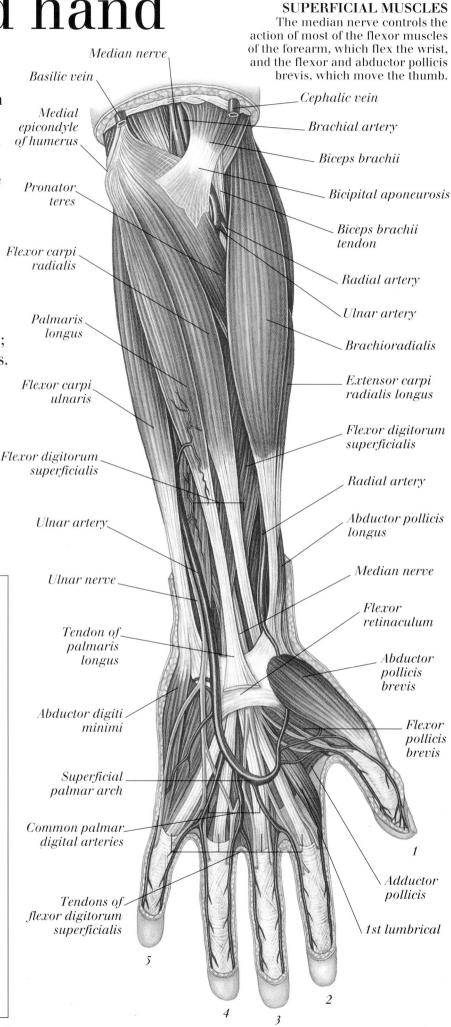

Median nerve
Basilic vein
Medial epicondyle of humerus
Pronator teres
Flexor carpi radialis
Palmaris longus
Flexor carpi ulnaris
Flexor digitorum superficialis
Ulnar artery
Ulnar nerve
Tendon of palmaris longus
Abductor digiti minimi
Superficial palmar arch
Common palmar digital arteries
Tendons of flexor digitorum superficialis

Cephalic vein
Brachial artery
Biceps brachii
Bicipital aponeurosis
Biceps brachii tendon
Radial artery
Ulnar artery
Brachioradialis
Extensor carpi radialis longus
Flexor digitorum superficialis
Radial artery
Abductor pollicis longus
Median nerve
Flexor retinaculum
Abductor pollicis brevis
Flexor pollicis brevis
1
Adductor pollicis
1st lumbrical

5
4
3
2

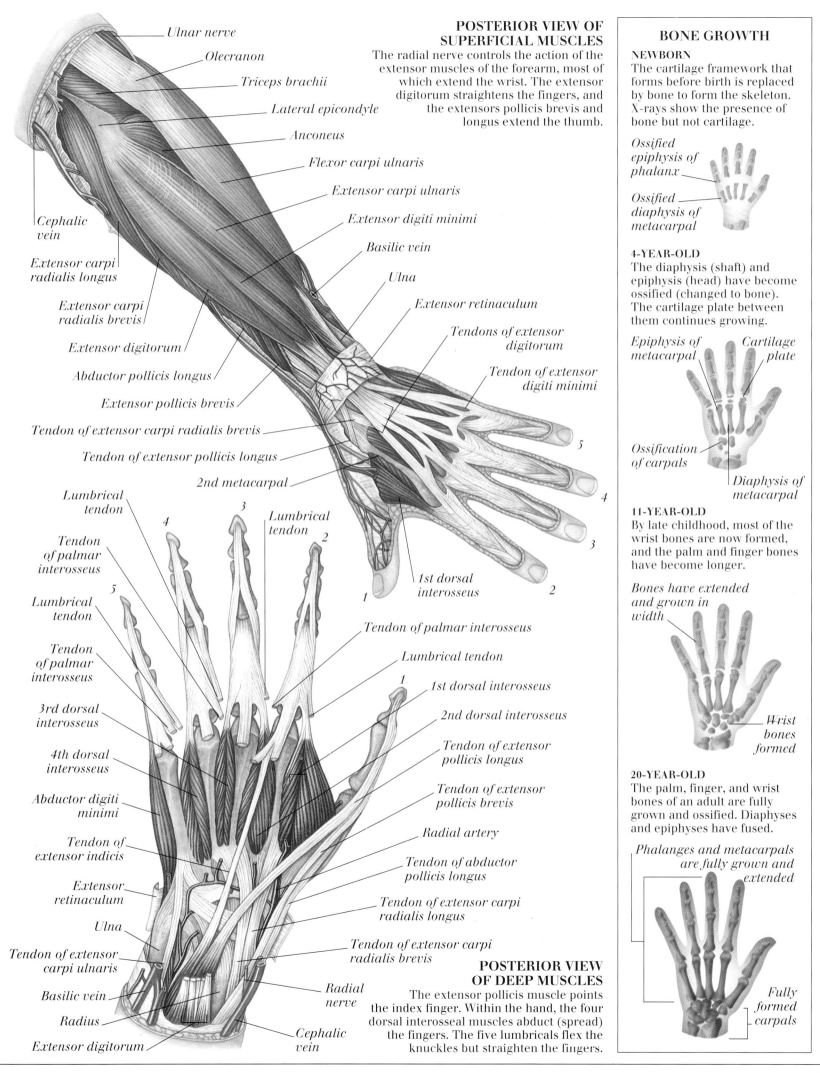

Ulnar nerve

Olecranon

Triceps brachii

Lateral epicondyle

Anconeus

Flexor carpi ulnaris

Extensor carpi ulnaris

Extensor digiti minimi

Basilic vein

Ulna

Cephalic vein

Extensor carpi radialis longus

Extensor carpi radialis brevis

Extensor digitorum

Abductor pollicis longus

Extensor pollicis brevis

Tendon of extensor carpi radialis brevis

Tendon of extensor pollicis longus

2nd metacarpal

POSTERIOR VIEW OF SUPERFICIAL MUSCLES
The radial nerve controls the action of the extensor muscles of the forearm, most of which extend the wrist. The extensor digitorum straightens the fingers, and the extensors pollicis brevis and longus extend the thumb.

Extensor retinaculum

Tendons of extensor digitorum

Tendon of extensor digiti minimi

1st dorsal interosseus

Lumbrical tendon

Lumbrical tendon

Tendon of palmar interosseus

Lumbrical tendon

Tendon of palmar interosseus

3rd dorsal interosseus

4th dorsal interosseus

Abductor digiti minimi

Tendon of extensor indicis

Extensor retinaculum

Ulna

Tendon of extensor carpi ulnaris

Basilic vein

Radius

Extensor digitorum

Tendon of palmar interosseus

Lumbrical tendon

1st dorsal interosseus

2nd dorsal interosseus

Tendon of extensor pollicis longus

Tendon of extensor pollicis brevis

Radial artery

Tendon of abductor pollicis longus

Tendon of extensor carpi radialis longus

Tendon of extensor carpi radialis brevis

Radial nerve

Cephalic vein

POSTERIOR VIEW OF DEEP MUSCLES
The extensor pollicis muscle points the index finger. Within the hand, the four dorsal interosseal muscles abduct (spread) the fingers. The five lumbricals flex the knuckles but straighten the fingers.

BONE GROWTH
NEWBORN
The cartilage framework that forms before birth is replaced by bone to form the skeleton. X-rays show the presence of bone but not cartilage.

Ossified epiphysis of phalanx

Ossified diaphysis of metacarpal

4-YEAR-OLD
The diaphysis (shaft) and epiphysis (head) have become ossified (changed to bone). The cartilage plate between them continues growing.

Epiphysis of metacarpal

Cartilage plate

Ossification of carpals

Diaphysis of metacarpal

11-YEAR-OLD
By late childhood, most of the wrist bones are now formed, and the palm and finger bones have become longer.

Bones have extended and grown in width

Wrist bones formed

20-YEAR-OLD
The palm, finger, and wrist bones of an adult are fully grown and ossified. Diaphyses and epiphyses have fused.

Phalanges and metacarpals are fully grown and extended

Fully formed carpals

55

Thigh

THE THIGH IS THE REGION OF THE LOWER LIMB between the pelvis and the knee. It is supported by the femur (thigh bone), which articulates with the pelvis at the hip joint to permit the thigh to move in most planes. At the knee joint, the femur articulates with the tibia to permit flexion (bending) and extension (straightening) only. The thigh muscles are used for walking, running, and climbing. Anterior thigh muscles are divided into two groups: the iliopsoas and sartorius, which flex the thigh at the hip; and the rectus femoris, vastus lateralis, vastus medialis, and vastus intermedius (known collectively as the quadriceps femoris), which extend the leg at the knee. The major posterior thigh muscles, which consist of the biceps femoris, the semitendinosus, and the semi-membranosus (known as the hamstrings) extend the thigh at the hip, and flex the leg at the knee. The gluteus maximus (buttock) muscle assists with the extension of the thigh during climbing and running. Blood is supplied to the thigh by the femoral artery, and removed by the femoral vein. The main nerves supplying the thigh muscles are the femoral and sciatic nerves.

ANTERIOR VIEW OF SUPERFICIAL MUSCLES
Most of the anterior thigh muscles straighten the leg and pull it forward during walking or running. The adductor longus and pectineus also pull the leg inward.

LATERAL VIEW OF SUPERFICIAL MUSCLES
The tensor fasciae latae muscle helps to steady the trunk on the thighs when a person is standing upright.

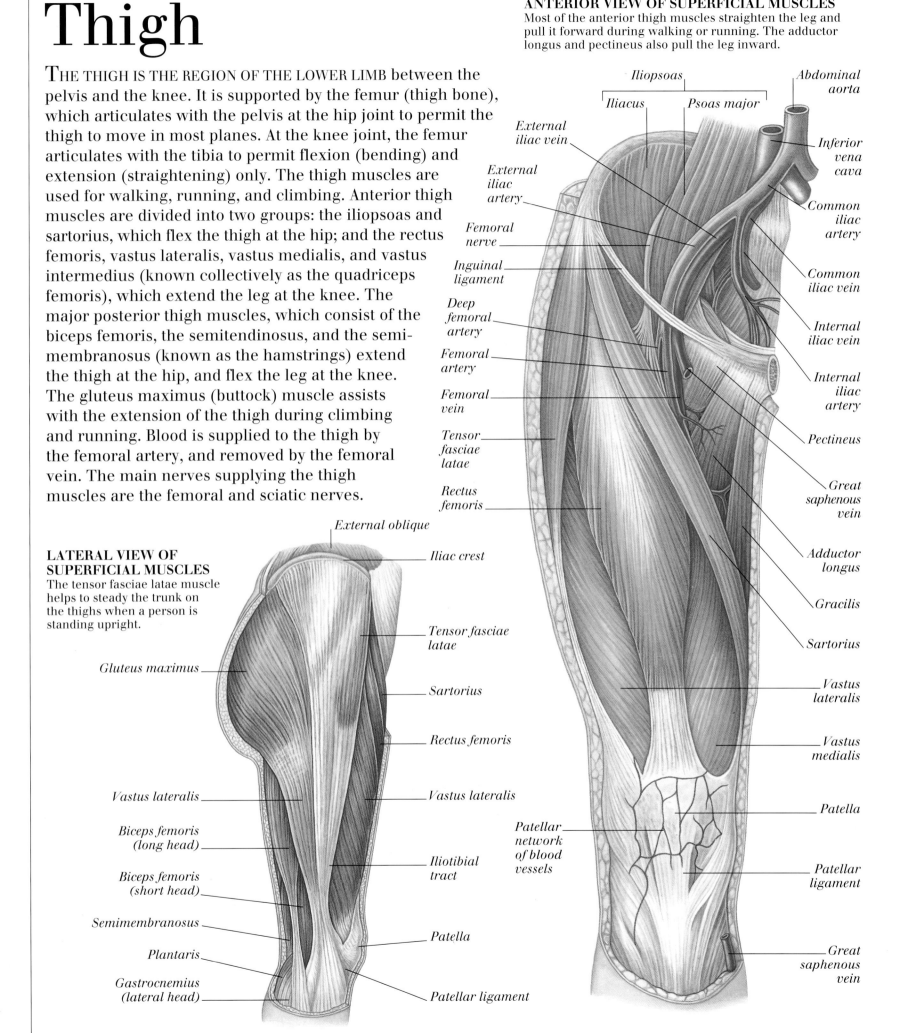

POSTERIOR VIEW OF SUPERFICIAL MUSCLES

The posterior thigh muscles produce the backswing of walking or running by bending the leg and pulling it backward. The gluteus maximus also steadies the pelvis, thus helping in the maintenance of posture.

POSTERIOR VIEW OF DEEP MUSCLES

During walking, the gluteus medius holds the pelvis parallel to the ground when one leg is in motion in order to prevent a lurching gait. The gemellus, piriformis, and obturator internus stabilize the hip joint. The adductor magnus pulls the thigh inward.

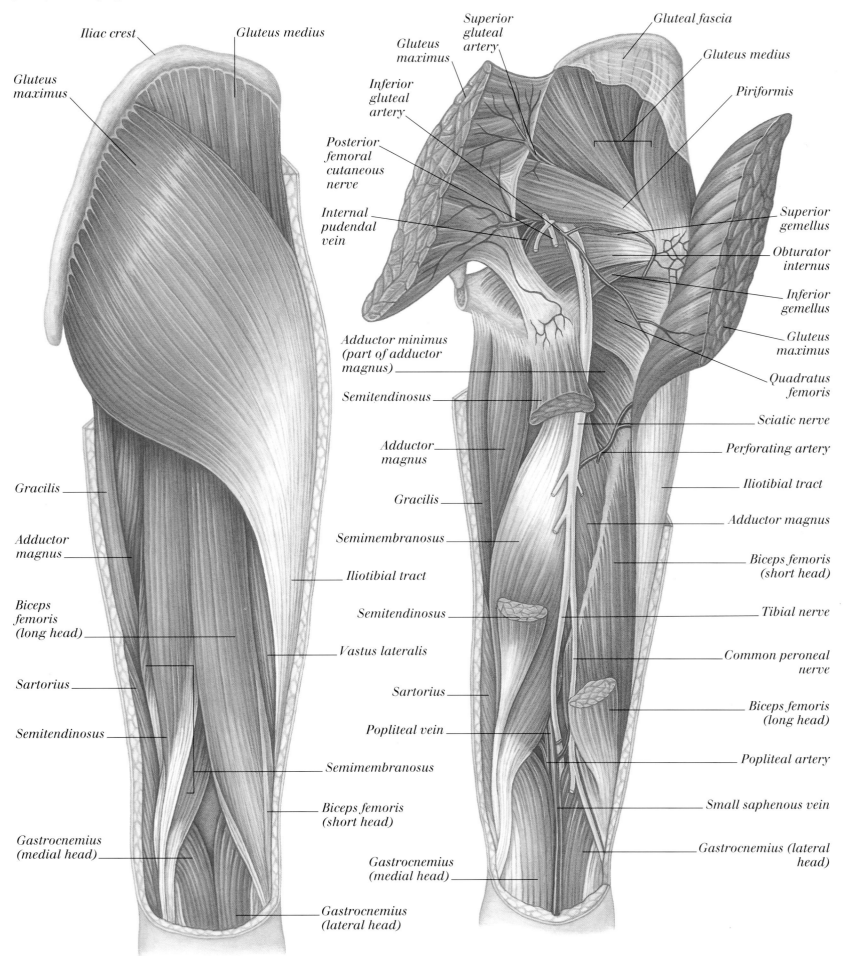

Iliac crest

Gluteus medius

Gluteus maximus

Gracilis

Adductor magnus

Biceps femoris (long head)

Sartorius

Semitendinosus

Gastrocnemius (medial head)

Gracilis

Iliotibial tract

Vastus lateralis

Semimembranosus

Biceps femoris (short head)

Gastrocnemius (lateral head)

Superior gluteal artery

Gluteus maximus

Inferior gluteal artery

Posterior femoral cutaneous nerve

Internal pudendal vein

Adductor minimus (part of adductor magnus)

Semitendinosus

Adductor magnus

Gracilis

Semimembranosus

Iliotibial tract

Semitendinosus

Sartorius

Popliteal vein

Gastrocnemius (medial head)

Gluteal fascia

Gluteus medius

Piriformis

Superior gemellus

Obturator internus

Inferior gemellus

Gluteus maximus

Quadratus femoris

Sciatic nerve

Perforating artery

Iliotibial tract

Adductor magnus

Biceps femoris (short head)

Tibial nerve

Common peroneal nerve

Biceps femoris (long head)

Popliteal artery

Small saphenous vein

Gastrocnemius (lateral head)

57

Lower leg and foot

THE FOOT IS A FLEXIBLE PLATFORM that supports and moves the body. The skeleton of the foot consists of 14 phalanges (toe bones); 5 metatarsals (sole bones); and 7 tarsals (ankle bones), 2 of which articulate with the tibia and fibula (leg bones) at the ankle joint. The anterior leg muscles – which include the tibialis anterior, extensor digitorum longus, extensor hallucis longus, and peroneus tertius – primarily dorsiflex the foot (bend it upward). The two extensor muscles extend (straighten) the toes and the big toe respectively. The posterior leg muscles – which include the gastrocnemius, soleus, tibialis posterior, flexor digitorum longus, and flexor hallucis longus – primarily plantar flex the foot (straighten the ankle), providing forward thrust during walking and running. The flexor muscles flex (bend) the toes and the big toe respectively. The muscles inside the foot help move the toes and support the arches. Blood is carried to the leg and foot by the anterior and posterior tibial arteries, and the peroneal artery; it is removed by the anterior and posterior tibial veins, and the great saphenous vein. The main nerves supplying the muscles of the leg and foot are the tibial nerve and the peroneal nerve.

THE FOOT

The bones of the foot support the body on both flat and uneven surfaces, and form a springy base from which to push the body off the ground during walking, running, or climbing.

The primary actions of the muscles of the underside of the foot are to arch the foot and to stabilize it during movement. As the foot leaves the ground, the flexors bend the foot downward.

SUPERIOR VIEW OF BONES OF THE RIGHT FOOT

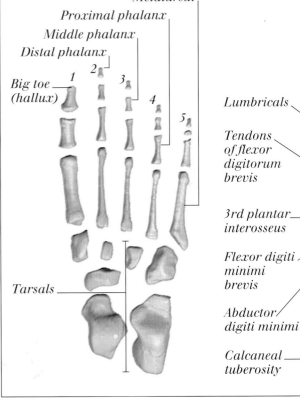

Metatarsal
Proximal phalanx
Middle phalanx
Distal phalanx
Big toe (hallux)
1
2
3
4
5
Tarsals

SUPERFICIAL MUSCLES OF THE SOLE OF THE RIGHT FOOT

Lumbricals
Tendons of flexor digitorum brevis
3rd plantar interosseus
Flexor digiti minimi brevis
Abductor digiti minimi
Calcaneal tuberosity

Tendon of flexor hallucis longus
Flexor hallucis brevis
Abductor hallucis
Flexor digitorum brevis
Plantar aponeurosis

1
2
3
4
5

ANTERIOR VIEW OF SUPERFICIAL MUSCLES

The main function of the superficial muscles is to dorsiflex the foot, preventing the toes from dragging on the ground during walking.

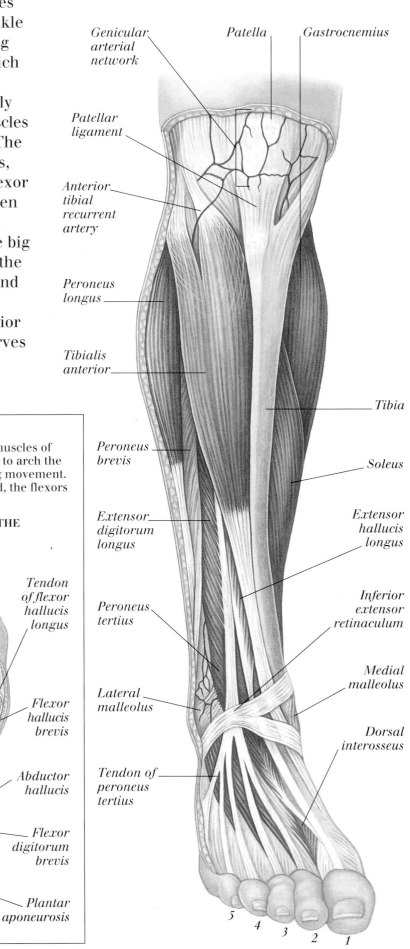

Genicular arterial network
Patellar ligament
Anterior tibial recurrent artery
Peroneus longus
Tibialis anterior
Peroneus brevis
Extensor digitorum longus
Peroneus tertius
Lateral malleolus
Tendon of peroneus tertius

Patella
Gastrocnemius
Tibia
Soleus
Extensor hallucis longus
Inferior extensor retinaculum
Medial malleolus
Dorsal interosseus

5
4
3
2
1

POSTERIOR VIEW OF SUPERFICIAL MUSCLES

The major superficial muscles – the gastrocnemius and soleus – act by pulling on the calcaneal (heel) bone to plantar flex the foot during walking or running.

MUSCLES AND TENDONS OF ANKLE AND FOOT

Long tendons extend into the foot from the extensor digitorum longus and extensor hallucis longus muscles. These work to straighten the toes, with the assistance of the smaller extensor muscles inside the foot.

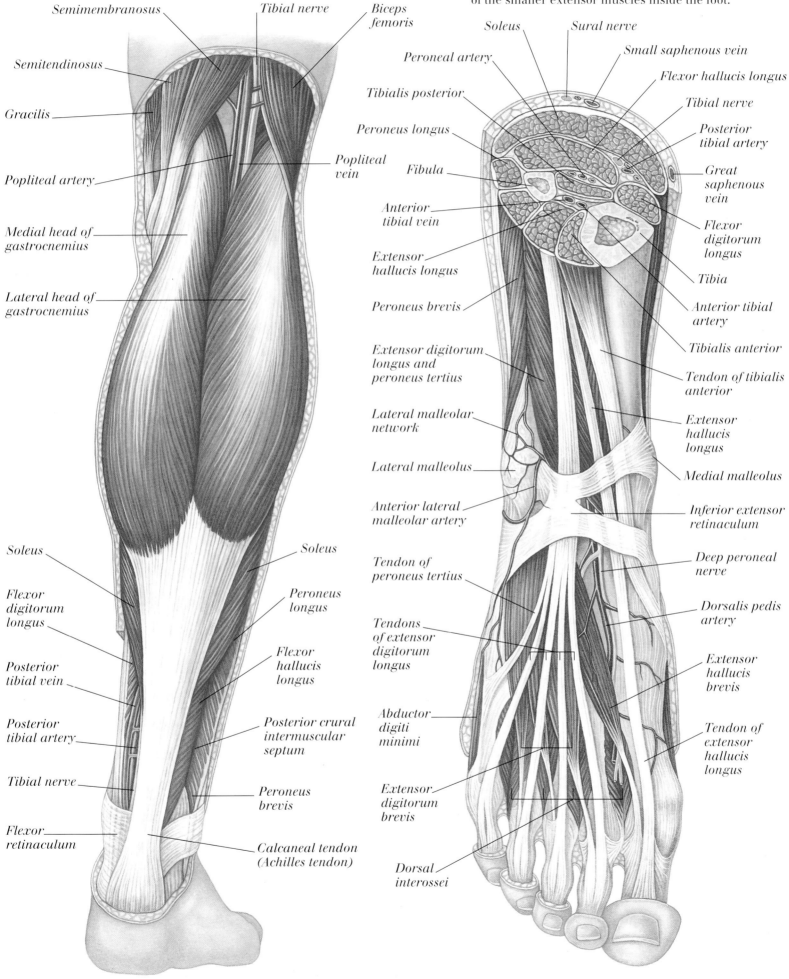

Semimembranosus

Tibial nerve

Biceps femoris

Semitendinosus

Gracilis

Popliteal artery

Popliteal vein

Medial head of gastrocnemius

Lateral head of gastrocnemius

Soleus

Soleus

Flexor digitorum longus

Peroneus longus

Posterior tibial vein

Flexor hallucis longus

Posterior tibial artery

Posterior crural intermuscular septum

Tibial nerve

Peroneus brevis

Flexor retinaculum

Calcaneal tendon (Achilles tendon)

Soleus

Sural nerve

Small saphenous vein

Peroneal artery

Flexor hallucis longus

Tibialis posterior

Tibial nerve

Peroneus longus

Posterior tibial artery

Fibula

Great saphenous vein

Anterior tibial vein

Flexor digitorum longus

Extensor hallucis longus

Tibia

Peroneus brevis

Anterior tibial artery

Extensor digitorum longus and peroneus tertius

Tibialis anterior

Tendon of tibialis anterior

Lateral malleolar network

Extensor hallucis longus

Lateral malleolus

Medial malleolus

Anterior lateral malleolar artery

Inferior extensor retinaculum

Tendon of peroneus tertius

Deep peroneal nerve

Tendons of extensor digitorum longus

Dorsalis pedis artery

Abductor digiti minimi

Extensor hallucis brevis

Extensor digitorum brevis

Tendon of extensor hallucis longus

Dorsal interossei

Index

Acknowledgments

Dorling Kindersley would like to thank:
Claire Naylor, Laura Owen, Simon Murrell for additional design assistance, and Caroline Hunt for additional editorial assistance.

Special thanks to Richard Greenland in DK Multimedia, and Richard Walker for his patience and cooperation.

The author wishes to thank Paul, Kirstie and the team at Dorling Kindersley for their dedication, hard work, and good humor.